Alice Lloyd Free

The Progressive Cook Book

Alice Lloyd Free

The Progressive Cook Book

ISBN/EAN: 9783744789110

Printed in Europe, USA, Canada, Australia, Japan

Cover: Foto ©Andreas Hilbeck / pixelio.de

More available books at **www.hansebooks.com**

"Such Lovely Rich Cream,"

is every housewife's verdict upon trying her first can of

HIGHLAND
EVAPORATED
CREAM,

An ideal form of Rich Milk for Table, Nursery and Cooking Use.

IT NEVER SPOILS.

WRITE FOR OUR COOK BOOK AND INFANTS' FOOD CIRCULAR. MAILED FREE.

HELVETIA MILK CONDENSING CO.,
HIGHLAND, ILL.

"WE ARE STRICTLY IN IT."

Do you know that we are selling _more_ and a _better quality_ of goods for _less money_, than any other similar establishment in this State?

IF YOU ARE NOT AWARE OF THIS FACT

it is time that you are looking to your own interests and try our goods and prices. We handle everything in the line of

Groceries & Provisions.

A FINE LINE OF

CROCKERY, LAMPS, BAR AND HOUSE GLASSWARE,

and every other article you may think of, usually found in a

COMPLETE GROCERY STORE

WRITE OR CALL ON US FOR PRICES.

DONOVAN & SPEAR,
CASH GROCERY HOUSE,
BILLINGS, MONTANA.

BILLINGS BUSINESS COLLEGE,
BILLINGS, MONTANA.

MONTANA BUSINESS COLLEGE,
HELENA, MONTANA.

Sustain the following Complete Courses:

COMMERCIAL,

SHORTHAND, (*Benn Pitman.*)

TYPEWRITING,

PENMANSHIP,

ENGLISH.

HOME IN PRIVATE FAMILIES FOUND FOR STUDENTS.

Students who complete a course of study, and practice in either of these Schools, are capable of performing any of the duties of business life. None but the Best teachers employed. Terms reasonable. Send for catalogue of information. Address

E. O. RAILSBACK, - - Principal.

Yellowstone National Bank,
OF BILLINGS.
CAPITAL, $50,000.

Regular Banking in all its Branches. Interest Allowed on Time Deposits. Safe Deposit Boxes Rented.

DIRECTORS: E. G. BAILEY, President, A. L. BABCOCK, Vice-President, G. A. GRIGGS, Cashier, DAVID FRATT, L. H. FENSKE, C. M. BAIR.

BUY A MEAL TICKET

AT THE

South Side Restaurant

WHERE YOU GET

A SQUARE MEAL

TIMES EVERY DAY.

MRS. S. VAN WAGNEN.

EPWORTH ORGANS for homes and chapels. No ag'ts. Shipped from fact'ry at special prices. Being Methodists, we prefer that orders be sent through our ministers, who may hold price until instruments arrive in good order and are found as represented. Catalogues free if name and address of minister is stated.

WILLIAMS ORGAN CO., Centerville, Iowa.

ENTERPRISING BUSINESS MEN. v

V. E. DAVID, M. M.
Teacher of Music.

Harmony, Counterpoint, Theory, Piano, Organ, Flute, Violin, Guitar, Etc.

P. O. BOX 194, BILLINGS, MONTANA.

O. F. GODDARD,

ATTORNEY AT LAW,

FIRST NATIONAL BANK BUILDING,

BILLINGS, MONTANA.

ALPHONSE HIRSCH,

BILLINGS, MONTANA,

Fine Dry Goods and Millinery,

LADIES' FURNISHINGS AND HOSIERY.

AGENT FOR BUTTERICK'S PATTERNS.   Near Grand Hotel.

W. R. FINCH

BILLINGS, MONTANA,

PHOTOGRAPHER.

CRAYON ARTIST.   ENLARGER OF PHOTOGRAPHS.

JAMES E. FREE, M. D.,

BILLINGS,

MONTANA.

HEADQUARTERS FOR
REFRIGERATORS, FREEZERS, GASOLINE STOVES.

❋ ❋ ❋ ❋ ❋

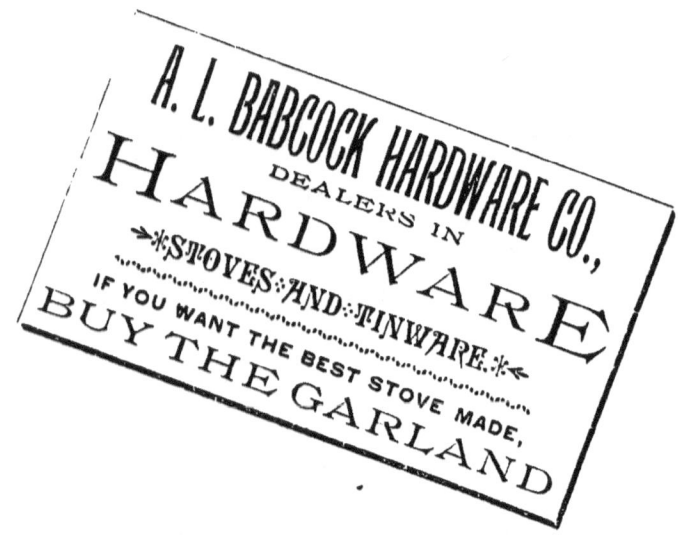

❋ ❋ ❋ ❋ ❋

FULL ASSORTMENT OF
HOUSE FURNISHING GOODS.

CHAPTER NO. 7707,
Loyal Epworth League
BILLINGS, MONTANA.

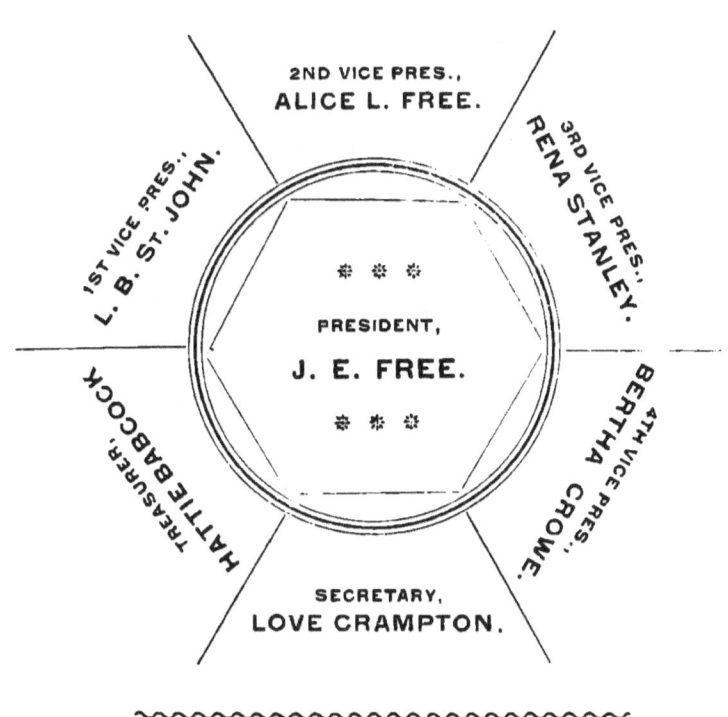

- PRESIDENT, J. E. FREE.
- 1ST VICE PRES., L. B. ST. JOHN.
- 2ND VICE PRES., ALICE L. FREE.
- 3RD VICE PRES., RENA STANLEY.
- 4TH VICE PRES., BERTHA CROWE.
- SECRETARY, LOVE CRAMPTON.
- TREASURER, HATTIE BABCOCK.

Meets Every Sunday Evening

AT 6:30 O'CLOCK.

EVERYBODY WELCOME.

THE PROGRESSIVES

BANNER SUNDAY SCHOOL CLASS.

First M. E. Church,

BILLINGS, MONT.

Rich in Good Works

◄ WEEKLY MEETINGS, SATURDAY EVENING. ►

ALICE LLOYD FREE, Teacher.

Bertha Crowe.
Jennie Kimball.
Hattie Babcock.
Love Crampton.
Lulu Browning.
Martha Hetland.
Etha Peck.
Maggie Peck.
Alice Holland.
Marguerite Jones.
Rena Stanley.
Elvie Crist.

Ella Mills.
Mary Kent.
Jesse Van Wagnen.
C. M. Holley.
Antone Hanson.
Chas. W. Goodall.
Chauncey Dodge.
G. W. Kimball.
L B. St. John.
Willis E. Gibson.
H. P. Ede, Violin.
W. O Allen, Cornet.

FIRST METHODIST EPISCOPAL CHURCH

BILLINGS, MONTANA.

Pastor in Charge, Rev. G. C. STULL.

Time Table:

Preaching Every Sunday, 10:45 A. M., 7:45 P. M.

Sunday School, 12 o'clock.

Class Meeting, Sunday, after Evening Service.

Prayer Meeting, Thursday Evening.

Epworth League, Sunday, 6:30 P. M.

CHURCH AND PARSONAGE

LOCATED ON

29TH STREET, NORTH.

YOU ARE CORDIALLY WELCOMED.

FIRST METHODIST EPISCOPAL CHURCH,
BILLINGS, MONTANA.

THE
Progressive Cook Book.

EDITED BY

ALICE LLOYD FREE,

FOR THE

FIRST M. E. CHURCH,

OF

BILLINGS, MONTANA.

Keep only thy digestion clear;
No other foe my love doth fear.
                    — *Mark Twain.*

When dinner has oppressed one,
I think it is perhaps the gloomiest hour
Which turns up out of the sad twenty-four.
                    — *Byron.*

WAVERLY, N. Y.:
WAVERLY FREE PRESS.
1893.

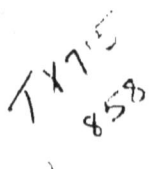

⋆DEDICATION.⋆

A square meal has overthrown empires.—*Exodus* 16:13, 14.
Ham has done wonders.—*Psalm* 106:22.
Bread may cause trouble.—*Isaiah* 4:1.

Therefore it is no vain thing that is placed on the altar of friendship, when I dedicate to my Sunday School class " THE PROGRESSIVE COOK BOOK."

ALICE LLOYD FREE.

THE PROGRESSIVES.

PREFACE.

A LITTLE BEFOREHAND.

The ordinary man is all right to vote, or to sharpen a lead pencil, but when he is weighed in the cook's balances, the verdict is, "guilty of murder in the first degree." Adam, *per se*, may have raised his eyebrows at Eve's perception of his humorous remarks in the Hebrew tongue. Yea, he may have sworn at her needlecraft, but the poor, miserable sinner was like the rest of us pan-handle brigadiers, an appalling failure with the rolling ladle and the soup pin.

Man has never been caught in the act of putting on his wife's apron and stealing softly down the back stairs at the cock of dawn. Peradventure he may steal a little about 7:30 A. M., and even exploit the kitchen fire. Then he threatens to rupture his bronchusses by shouting in a sliding scale,

"*SAY*, ARE YOU *ever* going *to* GET UP *THERE?*"

There are stirring times ahead of the American man; regular Frances Willard times; I might almost say egg beating, pie baking, cake cutting, bread kneading times.

The average Montanian is satisfied with his wife's cooking. He would be willing to take her to the World's Fair and expect to get a premium, and that is the spine of the mackerel for him.

To aid the women of the Yellowstone Valley to maintain their superiority, this book has been organized. Some of the things in it are fearfully and wonderfully made. Columbus might have gotten some points out of this book if he had been born in the right time of the moon.

The editor tells me she is sorry that her work is not more worthy of a place in her sisters' hearts. Her ulterior motive is to pay the debt which is hanging like a buzzard over the M. E.

church of this city. Debts get attached to places, and as Ruth said to Naomi, they seem to say, "Entreat me not to leave thee, or to return from following after thee."

Profits above five hundred dollars are to go to the editor. Glory will do, however, as well as money. The editor is grateful to her friends in Billings and vicinity (and the vicinity, in this case, has the big head) for their assistance. Whatever these friends hide in their hearts from these pages, it is hoped will be innocuous and good to eat.

The pseudonym of this book is intended as a compliment to the editor's Sunday School class. May their shadows grow as they eat of the fruit of THE PROGRESSIVE COOK BOOK.

J. E. FREE, M. D.

LIST OF CONTRIBUTORS.

- Mrs H. M. Allen.
- " W. A. Allen.
- " R T. Allen.
- Lillian S. Allen.
- Mrs. Barth.
- " L. M. Birely.
- " Walker Browning.
- " W. E. Barker.
- " R. K. Babcock.
- Miss Hattie Babcock.
- " Lulu Browning.
- " Maggie Boykin.
- Mrs. Andrew Campbell.
- " W. B. Chrysler.
- " C. M. Childs.
- " F. B. Conolly.
- " H. F. Clement.
- " M. J. Crampton.
- " D. Clark.
- " H. D. Claflin.
- " George Comfort.
- " R. R. Crowe.
- Miss Bertha Crowe.
- " Love Crampton.
- Jim Chinaman.
- Mrs Love Dill.
- " W. H. Donovan.
- " James Eccles.
- " J. W. Fish.
- " U. E. Frizelle.
- " J. E. Free.
- " L F. Fields.
- " Philip M. Gallaher.
- " J. R. Goss.
- " O. F. Goddard.
- " R. T. Hanna.
- " Alphonse Hirsch.
- " E. S. Holmes.
- " E. M. Hungerford.
- Miss Alice Holland.
- " Martha Hetland.
- Mrs. J. A. Johnston.
- Miss Jennie Kimball.
- Mrs. Lovett.
- " E. H. Lee.
- " Gib. A. Lane.
- " W. F. Leroy.
- " F. S. Mills.
- " Paul McCormick.
- " S. R. Miller.
- " Fred. Mashaw.
- " Frank McCormick.
- " J. F. Melcher.
- Miss Ella Mills.
- " Ruth Mills.
- " Mattie Murphy.
- Mrs. I. D. O'Donnell.
- " W. O. Parker.
- Miss Maggie Peck.
- Mrs. H. W. Rowley.
- " E. T. Ramsey.
- " G. C. Stull.
- " J. F. Sleeper.
- " F. R. St. John.
- " C. H. Sabin.
- " Charles Spear.
- " Fred Sweetman.
- " G. W. Shoemaker.
- " S. R. Salsbury.
- " Rachel Stephenson.
- " M. F. Sleeper.
- Miss Martha Shoemaker.
- " Rena Stanley.
- Mrs. Henry Terrell.
- " B. W. Toole.
- " Silas VanWagnen.
- " J. W. Vaughn.
- " Wells.
- " H. G. Williams.
- " B Woods.
- " A. J. Wilkinson.
- Miss Lydia Williams.

INDEX.

Beverages,	87
Bread,	31
Cake—Layer,	56
" Loaf,	63
Chinese,	49
Confectionery,	82
Cookies, Crullers, Doughnuts, Etc.,	70
Custards, Sauces, Creams,	46
Eggs,	29
Fish,	10
Frozen Desserts,	85
Fruit,	74
Meats,	15
Miscellaneous,	88
Oysters,	13
Pickles,	77
Pies,	50
Poultry and Game,	21
Puddings,	40
Salads,	37
Soup,	7
Vegetables,	24

Entered according to Act of Congress, the 10th day of May, 1893, by
ALICE LLOYD FREE,
In the Office of the Librarian of Congress, at Washington, D. C.

THE
PROGRESSIVE COOK BOOK.

SOUP.

CONSOMME.
Mrs. Rorer's Cook Book.

Four pounds beef, one ounce suet, one small onion, three quarts water, four cloves, one small carrot, a piece of celery, white of one egg. Put the suet and onion, sliced, into soup kettle, and cook till brown; then add meat and cook thirty minutes; add the cold water, cover the kettle and simmer for three hours; then add cloves and carrot, and simmer one hour longer; strain and stand away to cool. When cold, remove all grease from the surface; turn the consomme into the kettle; beat white of egg with half cup cold water; add it to the boiling consomme and boil one minute. Strain through cheese cloth, season, and it is ready to serve.

NOODLE SOUP.
Mrs. Rachel Stephenson.

Make a dough as for biscuit; roll and cut into strips, and put into the soup.

POTATO SOUP.
Mrs. Wells.

Peel and boil eight medium sized potatoes, with a large onion, sliced, some herbs, salt and pepper; press all through a colander; then thin with rich milk; add a lump of butter, and more seasoning if necessary. Let it heat well, and serve hot.

NOODLE SOUP.
Mrs. J. E. Free.

Boil meat in water. Take two eggs, a half egg-shell cold water, a little salt; mix stiff with flour and roll as thin as possible; dry by the fire and cut into fine strips; put them in with meat and boil half an hour.

MOCK BISQUE SOUP.
Mrs. J. W. Fish.

One quart can of tomatoes pressed through a colander, three pints milk, large table-spoon flour, butter size of an egg, pepper and salt to taste, a scant half tea-spoon soda. Put tomatoes on to stew, and the milk in a double kettle to boil; reserve half cup milk to mix flour smooth, and stir it into the boiling milk; cook ten minutes. To the tomatoes add the soda; to the milk add the butter, salt and pepper; then the tomatoes. Serve immediately.

CABBAGE SOUP.
Mrs. Rachel Stephenson.

Boil meat till tender; then take a little cabbage, cut it fine and put in; then take flour and rub one egg into it until moist, and drop into soup last. Season to taste.

CREAM OF POTATO SOUP.
From "Highland Brand Booklet."

Pare and boil four large potatoes. Heat one-half can Highland Brand evaporated cream and one and one-half pints hot water in a double boiler, with a slice of onion, one bay leaf, one stalk celery, and sprig of parsley. Rub smoothly together one table-spoon butter and two of flour, and stir into the cream while boiling, until it thickens. When the potatoes are done, drain free of all water, sprinkle with salt and stand back a moment to dry; then mash until light and free from lumps. Add the cream gradually to the potatoes, and press the whole through a sieve. Season with salt and pepper and it is ready to serve.

TOMATO SOUP.
Mrs. Paul McCormick.

One can of tomatoes, one can of water; boil for a little while, then rub through a sieve and return to kettle. Take one egg and a table-spoon cream and stir in just enough flour so that when it is dropped in it will come up in little strings, like noodles. Just before serving, season well with Worcestershire sauce.

GREEN PEA SOUP.
Atwood & Steele, Chicago.

Cover a quart of green peas, or one can, with hot water; boil with an onion until they can be easily mashed. Cook together two table-spoons butter and one of flour until smooth, but not brown; add to the mashed peas; then add a cup of cream and one pint of milk; season with salt and pepper, and boil up once. Strain and serve. A cup of whipped cream added at the last is an improvement.

BEEF SOUP.
Miss Martha Hetland.

Select a small shin of beef of moderate size; crack the bone into small pieces; wash and place in kettle to boil with five or six quarts of cold water. Boil until it begins to get tender, then season with salt and pepper; boil it one hour longer; add to it one carrot, two turnips, two table-spoons rice or pearl barley, one bunch celery, a table-spoon summer savory, powdered fine. The vegetables are to be cut into small pieces. After these ingredients have boiled fifteen minutes, put in two potatoes cut fine. Cook half an hour longer and serve hot. Garnish with sprigs of parsley.

TOMATO SOUP.
Mrs. H. W. Rowley.

Scald one can tomatoes; add one-half tea-spoon soda; let stand a minute, then skim off the top; add to this three pints boiling milk, and season with butter, pepper and salt. Pour through a colander and serve.

FISH.

SALAD FOR FISH.
Mrs. Fred Sweetman.

Three eggs beaten well; add two tea-spoons of black pepper, two of salt, and one of mustard, three table-spoons of melted butter, six ounces of cream and one coffee cup of vinegar. Cook in a custard until thick as cream. Set away to cool; then pour it over the fish. This salad is fine for salmon.

BROILED MACKEREL.
Miss Bertha Crowe.

Wash and wipe the fish well; grease gridiron and place the fish on it and broil well over hot coals, until both sides are well browned; then remove to a hot platter; butter it slightly; salt and pepper and serve quickly.

SCALLOPED SALMON.
Mrs. Paul McCormick.

Take a can of salmon, and pick out the bones, and put in butter and a little cream; heat it on the stove, then put in a baking-dish layers of bread crumbs and fish with salt and pepper, and enough cream to moisten. Bake slowly half an hour.

FRIED FISH ROES.
Miss Martha Shoemaker.

Wash the roes and cook them ten minutes in boiling salted water, with one table-spoon of vinegar; then plunge them into cold water. Drain and roll in beaten egg, then in seasoned crumbs. Fry in hot fat till brown.

BAKED FISH.
Miss Martha Shoemaker.

Clean, wipe and dry the fish, stuff and sew; cut gashes two inches apart on each side. Rub all over with soft butter, salt and pepper; put narrow strips of fat salt pork in the gashes, dredge well with flour. You want about one pound of pork; put what is left of strips, around the pan.

Dressing for the Fish.—One cup cracker crumbs, one salt-spoon each of salt and pepper, one tea-spoon each of chopped onion and parsley; one tea-spoon each of capers and pickles, one-fourth cup of melted butter.

CREAMED WHITE FISH.
From "The Ladies' Home Journal."

Boil the fish fifteen or twenty minutes, and take out the bones. Season with pepper and salt and a few drips of lemon juice. To each pint of this add a sauce made from four table-spoons of butter, two of flour, a speck of Cayenne pepper, and a pint of rich milk, in which a tiny bit of onion has been boiled. Mix the sauce with the fish gently, taking care that the flakes are not broken. Place in a baking dish, sprinkle with buttered crumbs, and bake from twenty to thirty minutes in a hot oven.

LOBSTER CUTLETS.
From "The Ladies' Home Journal."

Mince the meat of the lobsters fine; season with salt and spice. Melt a piece of butter in a sauce-pan; mix with it one table-spoon flour; add the lobster and a little finely chopped parsley; add a little stock also, and let it come to a boil; remove from the fire and stir into it the yolks of two eggs; spread the mixture in a shallow pan and when cold cut into cutlet shape, dip carefully in beaten egg, then in cracker crumbs, and fry to a rich brown color in hot lard..

CODFISH BALLS.
Mrs. H. G. Williams.

Cut the codfish in pieces when it has been duly washed and soaked, and boil twenty minutes. Turn off water, and cover with fresh from the boiling tea-kettle; boil twenty minutes more; drain very dry, and spread it upon a dish to cool. When perfectly cold, pick to pieces with a fork, removing every vestige of skin and bone, and shred very fine. When this is done, add an equal bulk of mashed potato; work into a stiff batter by adding a lump of butter and sweet milk, and if you want to have them very nice, a beaten egg. Flour your hands and make the mixture into balls or cakes. Drop them into boiling lard or good dripping, and fry to a light brown.

SALMON SALAD.
Mrs. C. M. Childs.

One-half head of cabbage, one-half can of salmon, yolks of two eggs, half cup of sugar, one tea-cup vinegar, French mustard. Beat the mustard, egg, and vinegar and let it come to a boil. Pour this over cabbage and salmon. Garnish top with hard-boiled eggs cut into slices.

SCALLOPED CODFISH.
Mrs. Paul McCormick.

Soak the codfish well and pick into bits, then put layers of codfish and sliced raw potatoes, and on the top lumps of butter; then pour over it cream or milk, to come almost to the top; bake about an hour, or little longer. It wants to be well cooked.

FISH CROQUETTES.
Atwood & Steele, Chicago.

Two small, or one large white fish. Boil, bone, and chop; add little salt, red pepper and onion. Make gravy of water the fish is boiled in; add milk, butter and flour; stir in the fish; shape into croquettes, roll in egg, then cracker crumbs and fry in hot lard. Garnish with parsley.

TARTARE DRESSING.—Take yolk of one raw egg, beat, add a little salt, red pepper, mustard, and mix well. Add salad oil until thick and let it stand on ice until needed; then add the juice of two lemons (or half a cup of vinegar), one table-spoon of capers, six small cucumber pickles chopped fine, and a very little onion. Serve cold with hot croquettes.

LOBSTER SALAD.
Mrs. W. Browning.

Take a can of lobster, skim off all the oil from the surface and chop the meat coarsely on a flat dish. Prepare the same way, six heads of celery; mix a tea-spoon of mustard into a smooth paste with a little vinegar; add two yolks of fresh eggs, a table-spoon of butter creamed, a small tea-spoon of salt, same of pepper, a quarter tea-spoon Cayenne pepper, gill of vinegar, and the mashed yolks of two hard-boiled eggs. Mix a small portion of the dressing with the celery and fish, then turn remainder over all. Garnish with the green tops of celery and a hard-boiled egg cut into thin rings.

OYSTERS.

OYSTER SALAD.
Mrs. Paul McCormick.
One can oysters, three eggs, four table-spoons vinegar, one tea-spoon mustard; pepper and salt to taste. Boil the eggs hard, take out two of the yolks and mash with vinegar, salt, pepper and mustard. Chop the rest of the eggs and lay around the oysters and pour on a little broth.

SMOTHERED OYSTERS.
Miss Martha Shoemaker.
One table-spoon butter in a covered sauce-pan, with a half salt-spoon white pepper, one level tea-spoon salt, and a speck Cayenne pepper; when hot, add one pint oysters. Cover closely and shake the pan to keep from sticking, cooking two or three minutes. Serve on toasted crackers.

FRIED OYSTERS.
Mrs. W. B. Chrysler.
Drain liquor from the oysters. Beat two eggs, or as many as required for oysters. Roll crackers fine, season with salt and pepper; dip oysters into cracker crumbs first, then into beaten egg, then back into cracker crumbs. Fry in hot lard as you would doughnuts.

CREAMED OYSTERS.
Mrs. J. W. Fish.
Measure oysters, and to each quart use one-half pint rich cream; heat oysters and cream in separate kettles, oysters in their own liquor, which, after they come to a boil, skim through and take out into another dish; then pour cream and liquid together; season highly with butter, pepper and salt, thicken with fine powdered crackers until like thin batter. Stir oysters in, and when boiling hot, serve.

SCALLOPED OYSTERS.
Mrs. R. T. Allen.
A layer rolled crackers in a buttered pudding dish, then a layer of oysters with seasoning of butter, pepper and salt. Repeat until the dish is full, with bread crumbs on top. Pour on the liquor mixed with a little milk. Cover and bake one hour; remove cover and brown before sending to the table.

PANNED OYSTERS.
Mrs. J. E. Free.

Drain the liquor from the oysters; melt in a kettle one-fourth pound butter; put in a little of the liquor, salt and pepper. When hot, put in the oysters and cook until the edges begin to curl. Pour into a hot dish on buttered toast.

OYSTER STEW.
Mrs. E. S. Holmes.

Put your milk, with a little water in it, on the stove to heat; put into it butter and a little salt. Put in the oysters, but do not let them boil.

MEATS.

HOW TO COOK HUSBANDS SO AS TO MAKE THEM TENDER AND GOOD.

ATWOOD & STEELE, CHICAGO.

A good many husbands are spoiled in the cooking. Some women go about it as if their husbands were bladders and blow them up; others keep them constantly in hot water; others let them freeze by their carelessness and indifference. Some keep them in a stew by irritating ways and words; others roast them. Some keep them in a pickle all their lives. It cannot be supposed that any husband will be tender and good, managed in this way, but they are really delicious when properly treated. In selecting your husband you should not be guided by the silvery appearance, as in buying mackerel, nor by the golden tint, as if you wanted salmon. Be sure to select him yourself, as tastes differ. Do not go to market for him, as the best are always brought to your door. It is always best to have none unless you will patiently learn how to cook him. A preserving kettle of finest porcelain is best, but if you have nothing better than an earthenware pipkin, it will do, with care. See that the linen you wrap him in is nicely washed and mended, with the required number of buttons and strings nicely sewed on. Tie him in the kettle by a strong silk cord called Comfort, as the one called Duty is apt to be weak. They are apt to fly out of the kettle and be burned and crusty on the edges, since, like crabs and lobsters, you have to cook them alive. Make a clear, steady fire out of love, neatness and cheerfulness. Set him as near this as seems to agree with him. If he sputters and frizzes, do not be anxious; some husbands do this until they are quite done. Add a little sugar in the form of what confectioners call kisses, but no vinegar or pepper on any account. A little spice improves them, but it must be used with judgment. Do not stick any sharp instruments into him to see if he is becoming tender. Stir him gently; watch the while lest he lie too flat and close to the kettle and so become useless. You cannot fail to know when he is done. If thus treated, you will find him very digestible, agreeing nicely with you and the children, and he will keep as long as you want, unless you become careless and set him in too cold a place.

BOILED MUTTON OR LAMB.
Miss Martha Shoemaker.

Wipe mutton or lamb, remove the fat and put the meat into well salted boiling water; put the bone side up and boil ten minutes. Simmer twelve minutes for each pound of meat. Serve with thickened gravy.

GRAVY FOR MUTTON.—To each pint of boiling water in which mutton was cooked, add one table-spoon of flour, moisten with a little cold water; one table-spoon vinegar, one-fourth salt-spoon pepper, one salt-spoon salt; boil five minutes, stirring till smooth; add two table-spoons fine chopped parsley or capers.

SCRAPPLE.
From "Parlor and Kitchen."

Take equal parts of lean and fat pork, from the heart, tongue and portions of the head. Thoroughly clean them and boil till tender. When done, remove bones and thicken the water with corn-meal until it is of the consistency of mush. Let it boil a few minutes and season with salt, pepper and summer savory. Chop the meat and return it to the mush, add salt and pepper to the taste, let cook a few minutes more. Dish out and keep in a cool place. Cut in slices and fry brown in lard, as needed.

BEEFSTEAK ROLLS.
Mrs. J. A. Johnston, Emporium, Pa.

Cut nice thin steaks and broil them slightly. Make a dressing as for roast turkey; roll the steaks, putting the dressing inside each roll; skewer or tie them neatly, lay them in a pan with a little water, spread over with butter, season with salt and pepper. Bake twenty minutes.

VEAL OMELET.
Mrs. Fred. Sweetman.

Three pounds of veal chopped fine, six crackers rolled fine, three eggs beaten well, one-half nutmeg, one-half cup melted butter, salt and pepper. Mix all well and pour butter over all. Cook one hour with a moderate fire.

BEEFSTEAK PIE.
Mrs. Alphonse Hirsch.

Cut two pounds of beefsteaks into large pieces. Fry them quickly; then place in a dish in two or three layers. Cut some onion and potatoes and put in the dish, strewing salt and pepper between the layers. Pour over it one pint of strong broth. Cover with a good beef-suet paste and bake two or three hours.

MEATS.

TO CURE DRIED BEEF.
Mrs. Lydia Williams, Wrightsville, Pa.

Take three rounds of beef, make a brine strong enough to bear an egg; one pound brown sugar, one table-spoon saltpetre. Keep the meat in the brine three days, then wrap it in paper, and hang in the garret till ready for use; then keep in the cellar.

PICKLE FOR BEEF, PORK, MUTTON.
Mrs. M. J. Crampton.

To one gallon of water, add one and one-half pounds salt, one-half pound sugar, one-fourth ounce saltpetre, increasing the rates to any quantity desired. Boil these together until all the impurities have risen to the top and have been skimmed off, Pour the same into a tub, and when cold pour over the meat, covering it entirely with the mixture, taking care not to put down the meat for at least two days after killing. For drying, take out the beef at the end of two weeks, dry and wrap in paper until used.

PIG'S HEAD CHEESE.
Mrs. R. R. Crowe.

Boil a pig's head and four feet until the bones drop out. When still warm chop fine and season highly with pepper and salt. Return to a kettle with one tea-cup of the liquor to every quart of meat. Cook a few minutes, turn into deep dishes, set in a cool place and when cold cut into slices.

BEEF HEART.
From "Mrs. Owen's Cook Book."

In the forenoon, put the heart into a weak brine. In the evening change to another brine, and next morning put it on to cook in boiling water; cook fully three hours. When tender, have ready a dressing of bread crumbs, mixed with melted butter, pepper and salt, and stuff the heart. Put it in an oven twenty minutes, to cook the dressing. Let it get cold and slice very thin. Season with pepper and salt.

VEAL CUTLETS.
Mrs. Wells.

Take the cutlets and remove all the bones; then chop them, first on one side, then on the other. Then take two eggs and beat them well; dip the cutlets into the beaten eggs, then in cracker dust and fry in hot butter. Season with pepper and salt.

FRIZZLED BEEF.
From "Highland Brand Booklet."

Cut away all rind from as much meat as you wish to use; then shave with knife or meat slicer. Put a table-spoon of butter in a pan and when hot, scatter in beef; place over a quick fire and stir with a fork to prevent browning. As soon as it is cooked, which will be in a few minutes, dredge in a table-spoon of flour, and add sufficient Highland Brand evaporated cream to make the gravy the consistency desired, and stir until well mixed.

VEAL POT-PIE.
Mrs. D. Clark, Emporium, Pa.

Stew your veal until soft and then cut it up. Make a rich pie paste; wash and pare some potatoes. Put in your pan, a layer of meat, potatoes and dough, which has been rolled out and cut into pieces. Then spread plenty of butter on top of layer, also season with salt and pepper; then another layer until all meat and potatoes have been used. Cover the top with layer of dough, pour liquor over the whole and bake in oven; baste often and do not let it get dry.

KALE BROSE (SCOTCH).
Mrs. Henry Terrell.

Have an ox head or a cow heel, one tea-cup toasted oatmeal, salt to taste, two handfuls greens, three quarts water. Make a broth of the meat and boil it until the oil floats on the liquor; then boil the greens and shred in it. Put the oatmeal with a little salt into a basin, and mix with it a tea-cup of fat broth. It should not run into one doughy mass, but form knots. Stir it into the whole and boil four hours. Serve very hot.

TO FRY BEEFSTEAK.
Mrs. J. E. Free.

Have your pan hot before putting in meat. Do not grease your pan, but lay meat in and cover with a lid; turn meat almost constantly and when done spread with plenty of butter, salt and pepper. Then take meat out of the pan and lay it on a hot platter. Put a spoon of flour in the pan and stir till smooth; then pour hot water on and stir till smooth and as thick as you like it. Pour this over the meat and serve hot.

BREAKFAST BACON.
Mrs. Paul McCormick.

Soak slices of pork in milk for fifteen minutes; then dip them into flour and fry; when done, slice some potatoes in the fat and fry. Serve in the centre of a hot dish, with a circle of the slices of pork around them.

MEATS.

FRIED LIVER.
Mrs. Wells.

Slice liver half an inch thick and put it into a dish; pour boiling water on it and let it stand till the water is almost cold; then take out the liver and roll it in one beaten egg, then in flour. Have at same time a pan of hot grease, and fry the liver in it. If you like, garnish the dish with breakfast bacon.

CORNED BEEF.
Mrs. M. J. Crampton.

First cover the meat for twenty-four hours with brine strong enough to float an egg. Take it out and wash it in cold water, then put it away in a second brine a little weaker than the first, in which you have dissolved three pounds brown sugar and two ounces saltpetre to a hundred pounds of beef. Should a scum appear on the surface before the meat is used up, the brine must be scalded and skimmed, and poured back when quite cold. The package should be kept in a cool but not damp place, with the meat always covered with brine.

ROAST SIRLOIN OF BEEF.
Miss Martha Shoemaker.

Six or eight pounds from the tip or second cut of the sirloin, wipe, trim and tie into shape. Lay the meat on a rack in a pan and dredge with salt, pepper and flour. Put in a hot oven with two or three table-spoons of drippings or a piece of fat placed in the pan. Put the skin side down first, that the meat may harden the juices in the lean part. When the flour is brown and the meat is seared, baste with the fat and reduce the heat. Baste often, dredge with salt and flour, and when seared all over, turn and bring the skin side up for the final basting and browning. Bake fifty or sixty minutes if liked rare; if liked well done, one hour to one and one-half hours.

BEEF OMELET.
Mrs. Harry Ramsey.

Uncooked round of beef chopped fine, two eggs, three soda crackers rolled fine, a little butter, suet, pepper, salt and sage. Make into a loaf, roll in crackers and bake. To be eaten cold.

DELMONICO HASH.
Miss Martha Shoemaker.

Remove the fat and gristle from mutton, lamb or veal and chop fine. To one cup of meat add one salt-spoon salt, one cup thickened gravy; heat quickly in a sauce-pan and pour over each slice of toast, which is buttered.

STUFFED HAM.
FROM "COOKING AND HOUSEKEEPING."

One pound bread crumbs, five ounces butter, one tea-spoon each of cloves, allspice, nutmeg, ginger, mace, celery, salt, one-half tea-cup sugar, two large table-spoons mustard, six eggs well beaten, and one boiled ham. Mix the above ingredients and moisten with cream. Gash the ham while hot, fill in with the dressing. Rub over it the white of an egg, sugar and grated crackers. Set in the oven to brown.

POULTRY AND GAME.

DRESSING FOR POULTRY.
Mrs. M. J. Crampton.

One quart milk, four eggs; make a batter as for fritters; then in the batter put a small onion, chopped fine; pepper, salt, and sage if liked. In your pan put lard, or butter, and when it is hot, pour in all the batter. Stir with a knife as you scramble eggs. It will brown lightly.

FRICASSEED CHICKEN.
Miss Martha Shoemaker.

Singe and cut the chicken, at the joints, in pieces for serving. Cover with boiling water, add one heaping tea-spoon of salt and one salt-spoon of pepper. Simmer one hour or until tender, reducing the water to one pint; remove all large bones, dredge with salt, flour and pepper. Brown in hot water. Put the chicken on toast on a hot platter; strain the liquor and remove the fat, add to the liquor one cup of cream or milk, and heat again; melt one large tea-spoon of butter in a sauce-pan, add two table-spoons of flour, and when well mixed, pour on the milk and chicken liquor; add salt, pepper, one-half tea-spoon celery salt, and if you like, one table-spoon lemon juice. Beat one egg, pour the sauce slowly on the egg, and stir well; then pour over the chicken.

MOCK DUCK.
Mrs. Harry Ramsey.

One pound of beef steak; salt and pepper either side; prepare bread as for turkey dressing. Sew up and roast one hour.

PRAIRIE CHICKENS STEAMED AND BAKED.
From "Mrs Owen's Cook Book."

Stuff them, after cleaning, with a dressing made of bread crumbs and seasoning of pepper and salt mixed with melted butter. Sage, onion or summer savory may be added if liked. Secure the fowl firmly with needle and twine. Steam in a steamer until tender, then remove to a dripping pan; dredge with flour, pepper and salt, and brown in the oven; baste with melted butter; garnish with parsley and lumps of current jelly.

CHICKEN PIE WITH OYSTERS.
From "Cooking and Housekeeping."
Boil a good sized chicken until tender; drain the liquor from a quart of oysters; line the sides and bottom of a large, round pan, with crust; put in a layer of oysters, then of chicken, till the pan is full. Season with pepper, salt, bits of butter and the oyster liquor; add some of the chicken liquor, cover with a crust and bake. Serve with sliced lemon.

CHICKEN CROQUETTES.
Atwood & Steele, Chicago.
One chicken, one set of sweet-breads, one-half pint milk, one table-spoon butter, two or three slices onion, two table-spoons flour. Boil the chicken and sweet-breads until quite tender, and when cold remove skin and chop together, very fine. Fry the slices of onion in a little butter until quite brown, and then pour over them a portion of the milk to extract the juice, and strain through a fine sieve into the meat. Put the rest of the milk and butter into a stew-pan. When they come to a boil add the meat, the two table-spoons flour, chopped parsley and salt and pepper to taste. Stir the mixture while thickening. When thickened, set aside to cool, and when cold mould into forms, dip into egg and cracker crumbs and drop into boiling lard. Garnish each form with a sprig of parsley and serve with or without sauce. Mushroom sauce is especially nice.

CHICKEN SALAD.
Mrs. O. F. Goddard.
Two chickens, two bunches celery to each chicken, one-half pint vinegar, two eggs, one table-spoon each of salid oil, mixed mustard, sugar, and salt, one salt-spoon Cayenne pepper. Beat the eggs and vinegar together until quite thick; then beat the oil, mustard and Cayenne pepper together and stir into it. Add the celery just before using.

WILD DUCKS ROASTED.
From "Mrs. Owen's Cook Book."
Prepare for roasting the same as any fowl. Parboil for fifteen minutes with an onion in the water, and the strong flavor that is sometimes disagreeable in wild ducks will have disappeared. Stuff with bread crumbs, a minced onion, season with salt, pepper and sage, and roast till tender. Use butter plentifully in basting. A half hour will suffice for young ducks.

ROAST TURKEY—OYSTER STUFFING.
From "The Ladies' Home Journal."

Select a young hen turkey, singe, draw, and clean thoroughly. Stuff with the following: Mince a dozen large oysters fine; add to them two cups bread crumbs, and a table-spoon parsley, salt and pepper and moisten with table-spoon of butter. Put two slices bacon in a pan, and after rubbing the breast of the turkey well with butter, lay it upon the bacon; roast in a hot oven, allowing from twelve to fifteen minutes to the pound. Baste frequently. Garnish with parsley and serve on heated plater with giblet sauce.

PRESSED CHICKEN.
From "Cooking and Housekeeping."

Boil chicken in a very little water. When done, take meat from the bones, remove the skin, chop and season. Press into a large bowl. Add the liquor and put on a weight. When cold, cut into slices and eat with sliced lemon or cucumber pickle.

ROAST DUCK WITH APPLES.
Juliet Corson.

Pluck and singe a duck, draw it, wipe with a wet towel and lay in a baking pan; wipe a dozen small sour apples with a wet cloth, cut the cores out and arrange around the duck. Put pan into the oven and quickly brown the duck; then moderate the heat of the oven and continue cooking until the apples are tender; baste both every five minutes until done, then serve both on the same dish.

POTATO STUFFING FOR POULTRY AND GAME.
Miss Wistar.

Two cups mashed potatoes, a tea-spoon onion juice, half a cup milk or cream, a table-spoon each of butter and chopped parsley; pepper, salt. Many like the yolk of egg, about two to the above. Mix and beat well.

VEGETABLES.

STUFFED POTATOES.
Marian Harland.

Take large potatoes and bake until soft; cut a round piece off the top of each; scrape out the inside carefully, so as not to break the skin, and set aside the empty cases with covers. Mash the inside very smoothly, working into it while hot, some butter and cream—about half a tea-cup for each potato. Season with salt, pepper, a good pinch of cheese, grated, for each potato. Work it very soft with milk and put in a sauce-pan to heat. When scalding hot, stir in one well-beaten egg for six large potatoes, boil up once, fill the skins, replace the caps and return to the oven for three minutes. Eat hot.

RICE AND CHEESE.
Mrs. Philip M. Gallaher.

Put a layer of rice, boiled in milk, in the bottom of a buttered pudding-dish; grate upon it some rich, mild cheese and scatter over it some bits of butter. Spread upon the cheese more rice and fill the dish in this order, having rice at the top buttered well without the cheese. Add a few spoons of cream and a little salt. Cover and bake half an hour, then brown nicely and serve.

FRIED EGG-PLANT.
From "Mrs. Owen's Cook Book."

Pare and cut into slices half an inch thick. Sprinkle a little salt on each slice and press down for an hour; then rinse in clear water and dry well in a towel. Dip in egg and rolled crackers and fry a nice brown in hot butter or lard. Season more if required.

POTATO PIE.
Mrs. M. J. Crampton.

Prepare mashed potatoes as for the table. Use any cold meat, stew, or fricassee of fish or poultry, removing all bones; line the bottom and sides of a baking dish with the potato; put the meat within, highly seasoned; cover it with potato. There should be sauce to moisten the meat. Brush the top with beaten egg. Brown the pie in the oven and serve hot in same dish in which it was baked.

STEAMED RICE.
Miss Martha Shoemaker.

One cup rice, one-half tea-spoon salt, two cups boiling water or three cups milk. Pick over and wash the rice in three or four waters, put with milk and salt, in the upper part of the boiler. Steam for thirty minutes, or until soft. Serve as a dessert with boiled custard or hard sauce.

GREEN CORN PUDDING.
Marian Harland.

One quart milk, five eggs, two table-spoons white sugar, one dozen large ears of corn. Grate corn from the cob; beat the eggs separately, put corn and yolks together, beat hard, add butter, then milk, sugar, and a little salt, last the whites. Bake slowly at first, covering the dish for an hour. Remove cover and brown.

CREAMED SWEET-POTATOES.
Mrs. Wells.

Boil sweet-potatoes and when tender drain all the water off; then put on them enough milk to make gravy, thicken with flour, putting in a good sized piece of butter, two table-spoons sugar; salt and pepper to taste.

BOSTON BAKED BEANS.
Mrs. Fred. Mashaw.

One quart beans washed thoroughly and put to soak over night. In the morning put them in a bean jar; salt to taste; one table-spoon dark molasses, one tea-spoon black pepper. Put in your salt pork and fill with water; put in the oven and keep filled with water. Bake in the oven a whole day, or longer.

AUNT CORDELIA'S LEGACY.
Mrs. J. R. Goss.

One pint cold boiled macaroni, one pint stewed tomatoes, one pint finely chopped beef or mutton, one onion minced fine and fried in a tea-spoon of butter, one cup bread or cracker crumbs, one tea-spoon salt, one salt-spoon pepper. Butter a two quart pudding-dish; put a layer of crumbs at the bottom, then a layer of minced meat, one of tomato and one of macaroni; sprinkle each layer with seasoning. Alternate in this way until the dish is full. Put a small cup of boiling water to the fried onion, and after making a layer over the top with the rest of the crumbs, pour it over them. Dot with tiny bits of butter and bake an hour, or until well browned.

BAKED BEANS.
From "Parlor and Kitchen."

Prepare them as for boiling, and allow fifteen to twenty minutes longer to bake them.

POTATO CAKES.
Mrs. J. E. Free.

Take what mashed potatoes were left from dinner; beat two eggs and stir into the potatoes, also add a little milk, flour and salt to potatoes. Dip a table-spoon of the potatoes, after they have been well mixed, into hot butter and fry like fritters.

HOT SLAW.
Miss Alice Holland.

One-half head of cabbage cut fine, one table-spoon flour, one table-spoon sugar, one egg beaten; vinegar, salt and pepper to taste. Fill a bowl three-fourths full of water, butter size of an egg. Put all together and cook until thick, then put in the cabbage and cook a little. Take off and serve hot.

SARATOGA POTATOES.
Mrs. W. H. Donovan.

Pare and cut into thin slices on a slaw-cutter, four large potatoes; let stand in ice cold salt water till breakfast is ready. Take a handful of the potatoes, squeeze the water from them and dry in a napkin; separate slices and drop a handful at a time into a pan of boiling lard, taking care that they do not strike together; stir with a fork until they are a light brown color; take out with a wire spoon; drain well and serve in an open dish. They are nice served cold.

GLISSENS.
Mrs. Henry Terrell.

Six large potatoes grated and squeezed through a cloth; grate three cold boiled potatoes, two eggs and a little salt; roll into little balls like marbles. Put one quart milk on and let it boil; drop the balls in, a few at a time, so they will not stick; cook five minutes. They are nice fried when cold.

BAKED CRACKERS WITH CHEESE.
Miss Martha Shoemaker.

For about twelve Boston crackers, allow six table-spoons grated cheese, a level table-spoon salt, one-fourth salt-spoon pepper. Split the crackers and bake in the oven or toast on a toaster. Spread them with the cheese, return to oven and warm till cheese is melted.

PARSNIP CHIPS.
From "Parlor and Kitchen."

Cut parsnips into thin slices with a potato cutter; soak in cold salted water and dry between towels; fry in hot butter, drain and salt. Stir with a fork till they are crisp.

MACARONI PLAIN.
Mrs. Wells.

Take one-half pound macaroni and pour boiling water on it, and a handful salt; let boil tender; put in a colander to drain, then put in a dish ready for the table. Take two table-spoons butter; let brown, then roll four crackers and let them brown in the butter. Turn this over the macaroni and serve hot.

CHEESE TOAST.
Mrs. G. W. Shoemaker.

Cook three ounces of fine cut cheese, one well-beaten egg, one spoon of butter and a half cup sweet milk. When smooth pour over nicely browned toast.

BAKED ONIONS.
Marian Harland.

The large Spanish or Bermuda onions are the only kind usually baked. Wash clean but do not remove skins; boil an hour. The water should be boiling when they are put in, and slightly salted. Change water twice during this time. When done take onions out and lay them upon a cloth that all moisture may evaporate. Bake in an oven nearly an hour; when tender through, peel and put in a deep dish; brown slightly, baste freely. Serve in a vegetable dish, and after you have sprinkled with salt and pepper, pour melted butter over them.

BAKED SQUASH.
Mrs. L. M. Birely.

Cut the squash into pieces, scrape well and bake from one to two hours, according to thickness. To be eaten with salt and butter, like sweet potatoes.

FRIED CUCUMBERS.
Mrs. L. M. Birely.

Pare and lay in ice-water half an hour. Cut lengthwise into slices nearly half an inch thick, and lay in ice-water ten minutes. Wipe each piece dry with a soft cloth, sprinkle with pepper and salt; dredge with flour. Fry to a delicate brown in nice lard or butter.

CREAMED ONIONS.
From "Kitchen Companion."

Boil half a dozen onions in three quarts of water for one hour; pour off liquor and cut onions into small pieces. Season with salt and pepper; pour a pint of cream sauce over them Serve very hot.

FRIED TOMATOES.
Mrs. Wells.

Take large tomatoes, not too ripe, slice half an inch thick; roll in flour, fry in hot butter; garnish with fried eggs.

CORN OYSTERS.
Mrs. J. E. Free.

Grate six large ears of corn; two eggs, a little each of salt, cream and flour. Drop a table-spoon of the batter into hot butter; fry a nice brown on both sides.

MACARONI AND CHEESE.
Mrs. O. F. Goddard.

Boil the macaroni in water until tender, which will be about twenty minutes. Mix a dessert-spoon flour with a table-spoon butter; add a half cup milk, a half tea-spoon mustard, same of salt and pepper, one-fourth tea-spoon Cayenne pepper, four ounces grated cheese. Stir all together and boil ten minutes; drain water from the macaroni and pour over it the dressing. Boil up once and serve hot.

EGGS.

OMELET.
Mrs. Philip M. Gallaher.
Six eggs, one cup milk, one table-spoon flour and a pinch of salt. Beat the whites and yolks separately; mix flour, milk and salt, add the yolks, then the whites. Have a buttered dish very hot and pour in. Bake in quick oven five minutes.

EGG SANDWICHES.
Mrs. J. W. Fish.
Yolks of two hard-boiled eggs, mashed fine, butter, salt and pepper to taste; when a fine paste, spread on thin slices of buttered bread. It is improved by adding slices of chicken.

EGGS FOR TEA.
Miss Bertha Crowe.
Boil eggs until very hard, lay in cold water one-half hour, remove shells and cut each egg in two lengthwise; carefully lay on a platter of crisp lettuce leaves, sprinkle with two table-spoons vinegar; add one table-spoon salad oil to the vinegar if preferred.

EGG OR GERMAN TOAST.
Miss Martha Shoemaker.
One egg, one salt-spoon salt, one cup milk, four to six slices bread. Beat the egg and add the salt and milk. Soak the bread in this till soft. Have a pan well buttered and hot. Brown on one side, then put a piece of butter on each slice, turn and brown on the other side.

BAKED EGGS.
Mrs. M. J. Crampton.
Take a pudding dish, cover the bottom with slices of toast soaked in hot water, buttered and sprinkled with salt. Break as many eggs as needed into a saucer, taking care not to disturb the yolks, and put them on the toast. Cover the dish and set in the oven. In ten minutes remove cover, sprinkle with salt and a few pieces of butter. Brown for three or four minutes and serve hot.

PICKLED EGGS.
Miss Bertha Crowe.
Take hard boiled eggs, remove shells, and place in vinegar with few slices of beets. Season vinegar with cloves, salt and pepper.

HARD BOILED EGGS.
Mrs. Rachel Stephenson.
To boil an egg hard, boil it twenty minutes.

EGGS A LA CREME.
Mrs. G. W. Shoemaker.
Hard boil twelve eggs; slice thin into rings. In the bottom of a large baking dish put a layer of grated bread crumbs, then one of eggs; cover with bits of butter and sprinkle with salt and pepper. Continue thus to blend these ingredients till dish is full. Be sure that crumbs cover the top of eggs. Over the whole pour a large tea-cup of sweet cream and brown in the oven.

EGG SALAD.
From "Parlor and Kitchen."
Take as many eggs as needed and boil until perfectly hard—almost half an hour. Take out the yolks carefully; chop the whites very fine. Arrange lettuce leaves or cress on a dish, making nests of the whites and put the yolks in each nest. Sprinkle over the whole French dressing.

EGG BALLS FOR SOUP.
From "The Family Cook Book."
Boil an egg hard, remove the shell and white. Rub the yolk through a sieve and mix with the yolk of a raw egg, a tablespoon salt, a dust of Cayenne pepper, enough flour to make the mixture firm enough to roll into little balls between the palms of the hands. Throw the egg-balls into salted boiling water and boil till they float on the surface. Skim them out and add to any dish for which they are required.

CURRIED EGGS.
From "The Kitchen Companion."
Six hard boiled eggs, one cup stock, one-half cup cream, one tea-spoon chopped onion, three table-spoons butter, one table-spoon flour, one tea-spoon curry powder; salt and pepper. After cooking the onion and butter in a small frying pan for three minutes, put in the flour and curry powder. Stir the liquid until smooth, then add the stock, cream and seasoning, and cook for ten minutes. Quarter the eggs and place in a deep sauce-pan. Strain the sauce over them. Serve hot with toast.

BAKED EGGS.
Mrs. Paul McCormick.
Break eight eggs into a well-buttered dish. Put into it pepper and salt, bits of butter, three table-spoons cream and bake quickly until the whites are cooked. Serve hot.

BREAD.

SIX WEEKS' YEAST.
Mrs. J. Fleming Sleeper.

One quart flour, one table-spoon each of ginger and salt, one-half cup molasses or one table-spoon molasses and two of sugar. Pour strong boiling hop water on this; when cool add the yeast.

HOP YEAST.
Mrs. Silas Van Wagnen.

Two handfuls of hops boiled a long time, three or four potatoes grated and cooked in the hop-water after hops are strained, a little salt, one tea-spoon each of sugar and ginger, one-half cup soft yeast or two yeast cakes. Put away in a jar.

BREAD.
Mrs. W. B. Chrysler.

YEAST.—Two quarts potatoes, pare, cut in small slices and boil; then mash, and add one quart each of boiling water and cold water. When luke-warm add one-half cup sugar, one-fourth cup salt, one and one-half cups flour and one pint warm water. Stir this together with two yeast cakes, and set in a warm place to rise half a day; then tie in a jar and set in a cool place.

BREAD.—For four loaves of bread and a tin of biscuit, take two cups warm water and four cups yeast. Make this into a hard loaf and let it rise two or three hours; then make into small loaves. Let rise half an hour, then bake.

STEAMED GRAHAM BREAD.
Mrs. Sabin.

Three cups sour milk or butter-milk, one-half cup sour cream or two table-spoons melted butter, one-half cup molasses, one cup boiled pumpkin or one-half cup sugar, one and one-half cups wheat flour, two cups graham flour, two cups Indian meal, one tea-spoon each of soda and salt. One-half cup raisins added makes a good pudding to be eaten with sweet sauce.

BREAD.
Mrs. Rachel Stephenson.

Cook two potatoes in one quart of water; one yeast-cake for four loaves of bread. Set sponge over night, and in the morning knead it three different times. Put into pans and let it rise; then bake.

BREAD OR RAISED CAKE.
Mrs. Geo. C. Stull.

Two cups raised dough; beat into it two-thirds cup butter and two cups sugar, creamed together; three eggs well beaten, one even tea-spoon soda dissolved in two table-spoons milk, half a nutmeg grated, one table-spoon cinnamon, one tea-spoon cloves, one cup raisins. Mix all well together; put in the beaten whites of eggs and raisins last. Beat all hard for several minutes; put in buttered pans and let stand half an hour to rise again before baking. Bake in moderate oven.

CORN BREAD.
Miss Maggie Boykin.

One quart Indian meal, one tea-spoon soda, one pint butter-milk. Make a thin batter and bake in a hot oven fifteen minutes.

ROLLS.
Mrs. Rachel Stephenson.

For two dozen rolls take one or two eggs, one quart sweet milk, one-half cup sugar, half cup butter. Let it rise and knead three times. Make into rolls and bake.

GRAHAM GEMS.
Mrs. Walker Browning.

Two cups graham flour, one cup wheat flour, two tea-spoons baking powder, a table-spoon sugar, one of salt and one well beaten egg. Mix with enough sweet milk to make a thin batter; beat it well. Bake in gem irons. Have the irons well greased; fill two-thirds full and bake in a hot oven.

WAFFLES.
Miss Alice Holland.

One-half cup butter, one quart flour, three tea-spoons baking powder, a little salt. Rub the butter into the flour; beat the eggs stiff and put into the flour; add one quart of milk.

BROWN BREAD.
Mrs Lovett.

Three cups butter-milk or sour milk, five and one-half cups graham flour, one cup molasses, two table-spoons shortening, two tea-spoons soda, a little salt. Bake from three to five hours in a moderate oven.

RICE MUFFINS.
Mrs. H. T. Ramsey.

Two cups flour, one cup rice, two cups milk, two eggs, two heaping tea-spoons baking powder, a little salt. The oven must be very hot.

BREAD.
Mrs. F. R. St. John.

Take one magic yeast cake and put it to soak in a little water at two o'clock in the afternoon; when dissolved, stir in flour for a thin batter and let it rise. When light, have one pint of scalded milk and the same of water, and make your sponge; put in salt and a little sugar. Let rise until bed time, then mix it hard, knead well, and cover until morning. Mix down two or three times and put into tins and let it rise; then bake.

ROLLS.
Mrs. F. R. St. John.

Pour one pint boiling milk over one quart sifted flour, two table-spoons sugar, two of butter, one of lard, and a little salt. When luke-warm add one-half cup yeast sponge and let it stand over night. In the morning knead it soft enough for rolls; when light roll thin, cut with biscuit cutter; spread butter on one end and fold over. Let rise and bake.

CORN BREAD.
Mrs. Rachel Stephenson.

Put your corn-meal into an iron pot; scald one-third and wet the rest with warm water. Keep warm until it rises. Take one-third and put into it an egg, a little sugar, pinch of soda and a little salt. Put into the oven and bake. The balance can be used at any other time.

BUNS.
Mrs. Fred Sweetman.

Break one egg in a cup sweet milk; mix one-half cup each of yeast, butter and sugar, enough flour to make a soft dough; flavor with nutmeg. Let it rise again in pans; bake, and when nearly done glaze with a little molasses and milk.

CORN-MEAL PANCAKES.
Mrs. Philip M. Gallaher.

One pint sour milk, one tea-spoon soda, one cup flour and one of meal, a little salt, and two eggs; whites and yolks beaten separately and whites added last.

SALT-RISING BREAD.
Mrs. Henry Terrell.

One small half tea-spoon each of soda and salt, one table-spoon sugar, one quart water. Stir thick with flour and set in warm water and let rise all day; mould into loaves and let it rise a half hour, then bake. This will make five or six loaves.

MUFFINS.
Mrs. Paul McCormick.
One cup milk, one of flour, one egg and a little salt.

WHEAT GEMS.
Mrs. G. W. Shoemaker.
One well beaten egg, two cups sweet milk, three table-spoons melted butter, two heaping tea-spoons baking powder, a little salt. Stir rather thick with flour, and have your gem pans hot. Eat with honey or syrup.

FLANNEL CAKES.
Miss Alice Holland.
Three eggs beaten separately, two cups sour milk, flour, a little salt, and one-half tea-spoon soda dissolved in a little milk.

CREAM BISCUIT.
Mrs. Philip M. Gallaher.
To one quart of sifted flour add two heaping tea-spoons baking powder and one coffee-cup sour cream, into which a scant one-fourth tea-spoon soda and a little salt has been stirred. Use sweet milk enough to mix up the flour so it will roll out easily. Have the oven hot and bake as quickly as possible. The above makes a superior crust for strawberry short-cake.

SWEET RUSK.
Mrs. J. Fleming Sleeper.
One pint warm milk, one and one-half cups butter, one cup sugar, two eggs, two table-spoons yeast; mix the milk and yeast and enough flour to make a thin batter and let it rise over night. In the morning add butter, sugar, eggs, a little salt, and enough flour to make a soft dough. Make balls of uniform size, set close together in a pan and let rise until light. When done, sprinkle pulverized sugar on the top.

CINNAMON MUFFINS.
Mrs. F. B. Connolly.
One tea-cup sour milk, one cup not quite full of sugar, one tea-spoon soda, one egg, one table-spoon cinnamon. Stir thick with flour and bake in gem irons. Very nice for breakfast.

RAG MUFFINS.
Mrs. W. O. Parker.
Two cups flour, two table-spoons lard, two tea-spoons baking powder, a little salt. Wet with milk, roll thin, spread with butter and sugar, roll thin like rolled jelly cake; cut in slices and bake.

ASTOR HOUSE ROLLS.
Mrs. G. W. Shoemaker.

Into two quarts flour cut pieces of butter the size of an egg, a little salt, a table-spoon white sugar, a pint of milk scalded and add while warm, one-half cup yeast or one cake. When the sponge is light, mould fifteen minutes and let it rise again. Roll out and cut into round cakes; flatten with the hand or rolling pin; place a piece of butter on top and fold each over itself. When light bake in a quick oven.

WAFFLES.
Mrs. Paul McCormick.

Two eggs, one pint flour, one and one-fourth cups milk or cream, one even tea-spoon baking powder, butter or lard the size of a walnut, and salt. Mix the baking powder and salt well in the flour, then rub in evenly the butter; next add the beaten yolks and milk mixed; then the beaten whites. Bake immediately.

BOSTON BROWN BREAD.
Lillian S. Allen.

Two cups corn-meal, two and one-half cups graham flour, one cup molasses, three cups sour milk, one tea-spoon soda, a pinch of salt. Steam three hours.

BAKING POWDER.
Marian Harland.

One ounce super-carbonate soda, seven drachms tartaric acid (in powder). Roll smoothly and mix thoroughly; keep in tight glass jar. Use one tea-spoon to a quart of flour.

CINNAMON BREAD.
Miss Wistar.

Two pounds dough, two and one-half ounces lard, one-half pint milk, three eggs, one salt-spoon soda, one pint brown sugar, two heaping table-spoons cinnamon. Melt the lard in the milk. Beat the eggs and add with the milk to the dough. Dissolve the soda in warm water and add it. Add the cinnamon. Bake as bread. Glaze with the white of an egg and sprinkle powdered sugar over it. To be eaten fresh.

CORN BREAD.
Mrs. Love Dill, Brooklyn, N. Y.

One cup Indian meal, one cup flour, two table-spoons melted butter, one egg, two and one-half tea-spoons baking powder, one table-spoon sugar, a little salt. Bake in a quick oven.

POP-OVERS.
Mrs. Paul McCormick.

Make by the above recipe for waffles, only stir in more flour, and bake in gem pans. They are very nice.

MARYLAND BISCUIT.
Juliet Corson.

Sift together one quart flour, one heaping tea-spoon salt; six heaping tea-spoons butter or lard; work in enough water to make a soft dough. Work and beat this dough, folding it over and over to entangle as much air as possible. When the dough blisters and breaks with a snap it is properly worked. Break off little pieces, prick them with a fork, and bake the biscuits thus formed.

SALADS.

MAYONNAISE DRESSING.
Mrs. W. H. Donovan

Beat one raw egg with a salt-spoon of salt until it is thoroughly smooth; add a tea-spoon mixed mustard made thicker than usual; when quite smooth add by degrees one-half pint olive oil, taking care to blend each portion of it with the egg before adding more. Dilute with vinegar until it assumes the consistency of thick cream. Lemon juice may be used instead of vinegar, or a few drops may be added with the vinegar.

SALAD DRESSING.
Mrs. Philip M. Gallaher

Beat the yolks of eight eggs, add to them a cup of sugar, one table-spoon each of salt, mustard, black pepper, a little Cayenne pepper and half a tea-cup of cream; mix thoroughly. Bring to a boil one and one-half pints vinegar; add one cup butter and boil again. Pour upon the mixture and stir it well. It can be kept for weeks by bottling when cold and putting in a cool place.

CHICKEN SALAD.
Mrs. M. F. Sleeper.

The yolks of three hard boiled eggs, the yolks of two fresh raw eggs, two table-spoons olive oil, one table-spoon mixed mustard, one tea-spoon each of salt and pepper, three table-spoons vinegar. Rub the boiled and raw eggs with the back of a spoon, add the oil slowly, next the mustard, then the salt and pepper, and last the vinegar. Cut the whites of the boiled eggs into rings, to ornament the dish, also garnish with the small tops of celery.

CREAM DRESSING FOR CELERY.
Mrs. J. W. Fish.

One-half cup cream, one-fourth cup vinegar or lemon juice, two eggs, a lump of butter, one tea-spoon mustard, salt to taste. Scald the vinegar with the butter, and pour over the eggs and cream beaten together, stirring all the time. Cook over water until thick. Let it cool and beat in oil to taste; a little Cayenne pepper. Cut the celery as for salad and pour the dressing over it. This is nice served as a garnish for fried oysters.

CREAM SALAD.
Mrs. H. T. Ramsey.

Chop fine one-half head of cabbage, add a small quantity of celery, stir into it a little salt and one-half cup sweet cream. Heat one-half cup vinegar; stir into it the beaten yolks of two eggs and a tea-spoon sugar. Pour this over the cabbage just as it goes to the table.

SALAD DRESSING.
Mrs. Charles Spear.

Four eggs, six table-spoons cream, two small tea-spoons ground mustard, pinch of Cayenne pepper, one salt-spoon of salt, three table-spoons sugar, a small piece of butter. Beat all together and set on the stove, then put in one-half tea-cup vinegar, and let simmer a few minutes.

POTATO SALAD.
Miss Lulu Browning.

Boil four large potatoes, peel and mash smooth; mince two onions and add to the potato; make a dressing of three hard boiled eggs, one tea-cup vinegar, one tea-spoon black pepper, one dessert-spoon each of celery seed and salt, one table-spoon each of prepared mustard and melted butter. Mix well with the potatoes and garnish with slices of egg and celery.

TOMATO SALAD.
Mrs. U. E. Frizelle.

Pare tomatoes with a sharp knife, slice and lay in a salad bowl. Make a dressing as follows: Work up a salt-spoon each of salt, pepper, fresh made mustard, with two table-spoons salad oil, adding a few drops at a time. When thoroughly mixed, whip in an egg beaten and four table-spoons vinegar. Toss up with a fork.

CABBAGE SALAD.
Mrs. J. E. Free.

Take a half head of cabbage, cut with a slaw cutter; cut very fine a little celery and add to it; sprinkle salt and pepper over it. Take a pint of thick cream, either sweet or sour, add vinegar and sugar to taste and pour this over the cabbage; then cut two or three hard boiled eggs very fine and add, and stir all well together. Garnish with hard boiled eggs cut into rings, and the top leaves of celery.

SALADS.

CABBAGE SALAD.
Mrs. E. M. Hungerford.

Beat two eggs with two table-spoons sugar, add a piece of butter half the size of an egg, a tea-spoon mustard, a little pepper, and lastly a tea-cup vinegar. Put these ingredients into a dish and cook like a custard. If you wish, you can add half a cup of thick sweet cream, but use less vinegar. Either way is very nice.

STRING BEAN SALAD.
Mrs. Wells.

String the beans and cut lengthwise; then boil in salt water, drain and add a sliced onion, vinegar and pepper. If you like them wilted, put a little bacon grease on the beans before adding the onion and vinegar.

CUCUMBER SALAD.
Mrs. U. E. Frizelle.

Pare cucumbers and lay them in ice-water one hour; do the same with onions in another bowl. Then slice them in the proportion of one onion to three large cucumbers. Arrange in a salad bowl and season with vinegar, salt and pepper.

POTATO SALAD.
Mrs. O. F. Goddard.

Chop cold boiled potatoes with enough raw onions to season nicely. For the dressing, take the yolks of three hard boiled eggs and salt and mustard to taste. Mash fine and make a paste by adding one dessert-spoon salad oil. Mix thoroughly and then dilute by adding one tea-cup vinegar, and pour over the potatoes. Garnish by slicing another egg and laying on it.

PUDDING.

CHRISTMAS PUDDING.
Mrs. Philip M. Gallaher.

One pound raisins seeded and cut fine, one pound currants thoroughly washed, one pound beef suet freed from strings and chopped fine, one pint bread crumbs, one-half pint sifted flour, one-fourth pound best sugar, one table-spoon powdered mace and cinnamon mixed, and two nutmegs. Beat nine eggs, whites and yolks separately, and add one pint rich milk in turn with the bread crumbs and flour. Mix with the sugar the grated rind and juice of two lemons or oranges; mix all together, stirring hard, adding the fruit after it has been dredged in flour. Steam six hours in a tin vessel covered tight in a kettle of boiling water.

A most excellent sauce may be made for this pudding in the following manner: Two cups sugar, one cup butter and four eggs. Cream the butter and sugar; beat yolks and whites of eggs and add them; lastly, add one cup boiling water. Flavor to taste.

LEMON PUDDING.
Mrs. G. W. Shoemaker.

One and one-half cups sugar, two eggs, two table-spoons cornstarch, two lemons grated,—rind and juice—one and one-half cups water, pinch of salt; stir well. Put in the oven until it stiffens, but not brown; dip out when cool and put a spoon of jelly with each dish.

QUEEN'S PUDDING.
Mrs. H. T Ramsey.

One pint bread crumbs, one quart milk, one cup sugar, yolks of four eggs, grated rind of one lemon, butter size of an egg. Beat the whites of the eggs stiff; add one cup sugar, juice of one lemon. Brown slightly.

ENGLISH PLUM PUDDING.
Mrs. Silas Van Wagnen.

One cup chopped suet, one cup brown sugar, one-half cup molasses, one and one-half cups currants, two cups raisins, one cup sour milk, one tea-spoon soda, two eggs, one tea-spoon ground cloves and other spices, to suit the taste. Steam four hours. Eat with any kind of sauce.

IMPERIAL PUDDING.
From "The Ladies' Home Journal."

Boil one quart of milk, one-fourth pound each of butter and sugar, and the yolks of twelve eggs. Beat the eggs and sugar together, then blend the butter and flour together and add to the eggs and sugar; then put in the hot milk; last the whites of fourteen eggs beaten to a stiff froth. Place the dish in a pan of hot water while cooking, and bake one hour in a moderate oven.

Sauce for the Pudding.—Two cups sugar, one table-spoon butter, and one quart strawberries. Beat the butter and sugar to a cream; mash and add the strawberries.

HONEY COMB PUDDING.
Mrs. L. M. Birely.

One-half cup each of flour, sugar, butter and milk; beat these well together, then add four eggs well beaten. Into one-half pint molasses stir one tea-spoon soda and add last. Bake in a slow oven. Serve with cream sauce or beaten cream.

ORANGE PUDDING.
Mrs. James Eccles.

Two large oranges pared, cut in pieces one inch square, and laid in a pudding dish; pour over them one cup of white sugar; then make a plain corn starch pudding, without sugar, and pour it over the orange and sugar. Let it stand and cool.

APPLE PUDDING.
Mrs W. A. Allen.

Five large apples, one cup each of raisins, sugar, sweet milk, and flour, one-half cup butter, two eggs, a little salt. Bake an hour and serve with sauce.

SUET PUDDING.
Mrs. F. B. Conolly.

One cup suet chopped fine, one cup New Orleans molasses, one cup seedless raisins, one-half cup sour milk, one tea-spoon soda, two and one-half cups flour. Spices to your taste.

RICE PUDDING.
Mrs. E. S. Holmes.

One cup cooked rice, one quart milk, one-half cup butter, one cup each of sugar and raisins, a little salt. Bake a long time and stir often.

COTTAGE PUDDING.
Mrs. W. E. Barker.

One cup sweet milk, two eggs, one cup sugar, two cups flour, three table-spoons melted butter, two tea-spoons baking powder. Bake half an hour. To be eaten with sweet sauce.

BATTER PUDDING.
Mrs. Charles Spear.

Four eggs beaten separately, one quart milk, two table-spoons corn starch or flour. Mix the flour with the milk; then put in the yolks of the eggs. After you put the batter in your pudding dish, add whites of the eggs and bake in the oven.

SUET PUDDING.
Mrs. E. S. Holmes.

One coffee-cup suet chopped fine, one cup each of molasses and sweet milk, three and one-half cups flour, one and one-half cups stoned raisins, one tea-spoon each of salt, cinnamon, cloves, and one-half tea-spoon soda. Steam two and one-half hours.

BAKED INDIAN PUDDING.
Mrs. H. F. Clement.

Boil one quart sweet milk; thicken it with three table-spoons molasses, four table-spoons sifted corn-meal, one table-spoon butter, one egg, a little cinnamon or nutmeg to taste. Serve with sauce while warm.

FRENCH PUDDING.
Mrs. G. W. Shoemaker.

One-third box of gelatine dissolved in one pint of milk; boil twenty minutes and add one cup sugar. Beat the yolks of four eggs and pour into the hot milk, stirring briskly. Again cook a little as for custard. Beat the whites of the eggs stiff and pour the boiling custard on them; stir fast, flavor with vanilla, and pour into moulds. To be eaten with one pint sweet whipped cream.

STEAMED PUDDING.
Mrs. Fred Sweetman.

One cup New Orleans molasses, one cup suet chopped fine, one cup sweet milk, one tea-spoon soda, three cups flour, one tea-spoon cinnamon, some nutmeg; add last one cup raisins, chopped. Steam three hours. Serve with currant sauce.

PORTLAND PUDDING.
Mrs. Philip M. Gallaher.

Three-fourths cup rice cooked thoroughly in one quart milk; then stir into it the yolks of four eggs, a small piece of butter, the grated peel of one lemon, and three table-spoons sugar, all well beaten together. Put it in a dish and cover with a meringue composed of whites of four eggs, four table-spoons sugar, and juice of one lemon. Brown delicately in the oven.

CHOCOLATE PUDDING.
Mrs. J. W. Fish.

One quart milk, one cup grated sweet chocolate, one cup sugar; heat the milk and stir in the chocolate while cooking. Beat six eggs, leaving the whites of three for a meringue; add butter the size of a hickory nut; flavor with vanilla, bake half an hour. Eat cold without sauce.

BATTER PUDDING.
Miss Rena Stanley.

For six cups, and put the fruit in each cup: Batter.—One cup sweet milk, one egg, piece butter size of an egg; make it of medium stiffness. Steam twenty minutes. Serve with sauce.

SNOW PUDDING.
Mrs. G. W. Shoemaker.

Soak one-half box gelatine in a tea-cup of cold water; pour on it one pint boiling water and set in a cool place, but do not let it harden. Beat the whites of three eggs, to which add three cups sugar, and juice of two lemons. Mix with the gelatine and pour into moulds. Serve with whipped cream sauce.

CURRANT PUDDING.
Mrs. W. H. Donovan.

One cup each of sugar, sweet cream and currants, two eggs, one pint flour, one and one-half tea-spoons baking powder, a pinch of salt. To be eaten with hard or liquid sauce.

BREAD PUDDING.
Mrs. Silas Van Wagnen.

Three eggs, one and one-half cups sugar beaten together; two cups milk, one tea-cup bread crumbs, one tea-cup raisins, one nutmeg, a little salt.

NO NAME PUDDING.
Mrs. M. J. Crampton.

Beat well the yolks of three eggs, add one-half cup sugar, a little salt, one spoon butter, flour to make a medium stiffness, one tea-spoon baking powder, and one cup seedless raisins; beat well together and steam one hour. Serve with a sauce made of one cup granulated sugar, one spoon butter, a little salt. Over this pour one cup boiling water; when it boils put in one spoon flour blended in three of milk. Boil one minute, flavor with lemon; remove from the fire and stir in whites of three eggs beaten to a stiff froth, with one spoon powdered sugar. The pudding is a golden yellow, the sauce is white.

LEMON CREAM PUDDING.
Mrs. J. A. Johnston, Emporium, Pa.

Beat four table-spoons sugar, yolks of four eggs, juice and rind of one lemon and two table-spoons hot water together. Let it simmer on back of stove until it thickens. Take from the fire and stir in the whites of the eggs, beaten to a stiff froth with two table-spoons sugar. To be eaten cold.

ORANGE PUDDING.
Mrs. Love Dill, Brooklyn, N. Y.

Peel and slice five oranges; one cup white sugar, one pint boiling milk, yolks of three eggs, one table-spoon corn starch made smooth with cold milk. When thickened, pour in the orange. Froth the whites of three eggs with a table-spoon powdered sugar; pour this over all. Set in the oven to harden.

COTTAGE PUDDING.
Mrs. W. Browning.

One heaping pint flour, one-half cup sugar, one cup milk, one tea-spoon soda dissolved in the milk, one table-spoon butter, two tea-spoons cream tartar rubbed dry in the flour; flavor with nutmeg and bake in a moderate oven. Cut in slices and serve with sweet sauce.

BAKED APPLE DUMPLINGS.
From "The Ladies' Home Journal."

Use tart apples. Make a paste of one quart flour, into which two heaping tea-spoons baking powder have been sifted, and also one of soda, one-fourth pound butter or lard, some salt. Rub well together and wet up quickly with water enough to make a stiff paste. Roll into sheets and cut into squares. Put with it before covering, a heaping tea-spoon each of butter and sugar. Arrange the dumplings in a pan half filled with water, into which melt one-third tea-cup butter and one tea-cup sugar seasoned with cinnamon. Baste frequently.

CABINET PUDDING.
Marian Harland.

One-half pound flour, scant one-fourth pound butter, five eggs, one and one-half pounds sugar, one-half pound raisins, seeded and chopped, one-fourth pound currants, washed and dried, one-half cup cream or milk, one half lemon—juice, and rind grated. Cream the butter and sugar; add the beaten yolks, then the milk and flour alternately with the whites; lastly, stir in the fruit dredged with flour; boil two and one-half hours. Serve hot with sauce.

TRANSPARENT PUDDING.
Mrs. Love Dill, Brooklyn, N. Y.

Six eggs, one-half pound each of sugar and butter; melt the butter and sugar together; beat the eggs well and stir in while the ingredients are warm. Pour into paste without top.

BAKED TOMATO PUDDING.
Mrs. Love Dill, Brooklyn, N. Y.

Butter the inside of a deep pudding dish. Put in a layer of bread crumbs, a layer of pealed sliced tomato, a small onion chopped fine; dredge with a little flour, pepper and salt, two table-spoons sugar. Continue thus until the dish is full, the top layer being crumbs, with small bits of butter. Put in the oven, keep covered for an hour, then uncover and cook another hour.

TAPIOCA PUDDING.
Mrs. Love Dill, Brooklyn, N. Y.

Soak eight table-spoons tapioca in one quart of milk till soft; then add two table-spoons melted butter, four eggs well beaten, spice and sugar to taste. Bake in a buttered dish. Serve with or without sauce.

CUSTARDS, SAUCES, ETC.

WHIPPED CREAM.
Mrs. J. E. Free.
Whip your cream with a fork. Sweeten and flavor to taste.

FRENCH CUSTARD.
Mrs J. Fleming Sleeper.
Beat four eggs separately; to the yolks add two table-spoons flour and one quart milk; let this come to a boil, sweeten and flavor to taste. Put four tea-spoons sugar and some flavoring into the whites of the eggs; beat very stiff. Drop this over the custard and brown. Eat without sauce.

COFFEE JELLY.
Mrs. G. W. Shoemaker.
One-half box of gelatine dissolved in one cup cold water, one cup boiling coffee, one cup boiling water, one and one-half cups sugar; let it come to a boil, strain and set in moulds to cool. Eat with cream and sugar.

LEMON SAUCE.
Mrs. O. F. Goddard.
One cup sugar, one-half cup butter, one egg, one lemon (juice and grated rind), three table-spoons boiling water. Put in a tin pail and thicken over steam.

CHOCOLATE CREAM.
Mrs. Philip M. Gallaher.
Two quarts milk boiled and sweetened, three-fourths pound chocolate scraped and dissolved in milk. Add the milk to the chocolate, stirring constantly; boil until you think it is cooked. Beat the yolks of four eggs and add to the chocolate. When cool, strain the whole and boil to the consistency of rich custard.

CORN STARCH BLANC MANGE.
Miss Lulu Browning.
Take one quart sweet milk and put one pint of it on the stove to heat; in the other pint mix four heaping table-spoons corn starch and one-half cup sugar. When the milk is hot pour in the cold milk with the corn starch and sugar thoroughly mixed in it, and stir all together until there are no lumps, and it is thick; flavor with lemon. Take it from the stove and add the whites of three eggs beaten to a stiff froth.

CHARLOTTE RUSSE.
Mrs. J. A. Johnston, Emporium, Pa.

Soak three-fourths box gelatine in one pint cold water; boil until it is reduced one-half. While this is cooking, beat together the yolks of four eggs with one-half pound sugar; strain the gelatine and when cool put it into the eggs. Whip one quart rich cream to a stiff froth; beat all together quickly and pour into a dish lined with cake.

CORN STARCH BLANC MANGE.
Miss Lulu Browning.

Take one quart sweet milk and put one pint of it on the stove to heat; in the other pint mix four heaping table-spoons corn starch and one-half cup sugar. When the milk is hot, pour in the cold milk with the corn starch and sugar thoroughly mixed in it, and stir all together until there are no lumps and it is thick; flavor with lemon. Take from stove and add the whites of three eggs beaten to a stiff froth.

LEMON CUSTARD.
Mrs. J. W. Vaughn.

One pint sweet cream, three eggs, one lemon, two-thirds cup sugar. Mix the cream, sugar and eggs together, then chop the lemon fine and put into it. Bake at once.

ORANGE CREAM.
From "Mrs. Rorer's Cook Book."

One-half box gelatine, one cup sugar, five oranges, one pint each of sweet cream and sweet milk, yolks of five eggs, Cover the gelatine with cold water and let stand half an hour. Whip the cream. Put the milk on to boil; as soon as it boils put in the gelatine. Beat the eggs and sugar together until light; strain gelatine and milk into them. Wash the boiler and return the mixture. Stir two minutes, then turn out to cool. When cold add the juice of the oranges. Place the dish in a pan of cracked ice and stir until it begins to thicken, then add the whipped cream. Turn into fancy mould and stand on ice to harden. Serve plain or with whipped cream heaped around it.

ORANGE JELLY.
Mrs. Charles Spear.

Soak one box gelatine in one pint of water and let stand two hours; three oranges and one lemon—take all the seeds out, the rinds off and add the rest, three tea-cups sugar; add one quart water and set on stove; then put in the gelatine and let boil five minutes. Pour into moulds.

BOILED CUSTARD.
Mrs. C. M. Childs.

One large pint milk, one dessert-spoon vanilla, small pinch salt, yolks of two eggs well beaten with five dessert-spoons sugar, two dessert-spoons corn starch dissolved in one-half cup milk. Put the milk in an extra pail on the stove, and when it almost boils, put in the other ingredients, then boil it thick. Take from the stove and put a meringue of the whites of two eggs well beaten with one table-spoon sugar, and lemon flavoring. Brown slightly in the oven. When ready to serve, put a spoon of jelly in each dish with the custard.

RICE SNOW BALLS.

Wash and boil two cups rice in one tea-cup water and one of milk, with a little salt. When the rice is tender, flavor with vanilla. Form into balls and place around the inside of a deep dish with a soft, rich custard. Serve either hot or cold.

WHITE SAUCE FOR VEGETABLES, ETC.
Miss Martha Shoemaker.

One pint milk, two table-spoons each of butter and flour, one-half tea-spoon salt, one-half salt-spoon pepper; heat the milk over hot water; put the butter in a granite sauce-pan and stir until it melts; add dry flour and stir quickly until it melts. Pour on a little of the milk and let it boil, and stir well; then add the remainder of the milk and stir until perfectly smooth. Then add salt and pepper.

CHINESE.

CHINESE FRITTERS.

Two cups rice flour, one-half cup sugar; scald him with hot water. Mix like bread, roll into balls, put in hot fat on stove, cook him like doughnuts.

CUSTARD.
JIM CHINAMAN.

Two eggs, one cup milk, three spoons sugar; have slow fire; no cook long, spoil it.

RICE.
BY A SEA CAPTAIN.

Wash him well, much wash in cold water the rice, flour make him stick. Water boil already very fast; throw him in, rice can't burn, water shake him too much. Boil one-fourth hour or little more; rub one rice between thumb and finger, if all rub away, him quite done. Put rice in colander, hot water run away; pour cup cold water on him; put back rice in sauce-pan, keep him covered near fire, then rice all ready, "eat him up."

SPONGE CAKE.

Four eggs, two cups flour, one cup sugar, little vanilla. Beat eggs separately, and put in whites last.

BROWN BREAD.
JIM CHINAMAN.

Two cups water, three-fourths cup molasses; mix with white and graham flour together; one-half cup yeast, a litttle salt.

GREEN PEPPERS.

Chop meat; cut hole, take out seeds, fill up, little salt; put in oven, bake. "Eat him up."

PIES.

PASTRY FOR ONE PIE.
Miss Martha Shoemaker.

One and one-half cups flour, from one-half to three-fourths cup butter and lard mixed, one-half tea-spoon salt, one salt-spoon baking powder. Sift the flour, salt and baking powder twice. Rub in the shortening until fine like meal, then wet with a little cold water.

FLAKY PIE CRUST.
Mrs. M. J. Crampton.

Roll upper crust thin; spread it with lard or butter, then scatter flour over it. Fold the crust on the middle from each of the four corners. Do this four times. Spread a little lard over the pie crust just before putting in the oven.

LEMON PIE.
Mrs. W. Browning.

The yolks of six eggs and two cups pulverized sugar beaten well together, two and one-half cups milk, juice of three lemons, a little salt. Mix well and bake with one crust. Spread a meringue of whites of the eggs and one cup pulverized sugar over top of pies and brown in the oven. This makes two pies.

LEMON PIE.
Mrs. H. F. Clement.

One cup hot water, one table-spoon corn starch, one cup white sugar, one table-spoon butter, the juice and grated rind of one lemon. Cook for a few minutes, add one egg and bake with bottom and top crusts.

GOLDEN PIE.
Mrs. H. T. Ramsey.

The rind and juice of one lemon, one cup each of sugar and milk, one table-spoon corn starch, yolks of three eggs. Bake slowly and frost the top.

PINE-APPLE PIE.
Mrs. J. A. Johnston, Emporium, Pa.

One grated pine-apple and its weight in sugar, one-half its weight in butter, five eggs, the whites beaten to a stiff froth, one cup cream. Cream the butter, sugar and yolks of the eggs until very light; add the cream, pine-apple and whites of the eggs. Bake with an under crust.

CRANBERRY PIE.
Mrs. Wells.

Boil the cranberries until almost done; sweeten and cool. Roll out pie crust, put in cranberries, and cover with strips of crust, twisting them before putting on. Bake quickly.

CHERRY TART.
From "The Ladies' Home Journal."

Line the pie dish with rich paste; sprinkle over it about a level table-spoon sifted flour, and a little butter. Pour into it the fresh cherries, stemmed and pitted, and sprinkle over them one-half cup granulated sugar. When baked, cover top with meringue of the white of one egg beaten to a stiff froth with one large spoon of pulverized sugar. Return to oven long enough to make the icing firm.

SQUASH PIE.
Mrs. Philip M. Gallaher.

One quart baked squash (Hubbard if possible) pressed through a sieve, eight eggs beaten separately, two quarts milk, two cups white sugar, one tea-spoon nutmeg, half tea-spoon cinnamon, and one tea-spoon salt. Beat all together and bake in under crust without cover. The under crust should first be rubbed with a well-beaten egg.

LEMON PIE.
Mrs. E. M. Hungerford.

One coffee-cup sugar, three eggs, one cup water, one table-spoon melted butter, one heaping table-spoon flour, the juice and a little of the rind of one lemon; reserve the whites of the eggs, and when the pie is done, spread them over the top, beaten lightly with a spoon of sugar; return to oven and brown. This may be cooked before putting into the pie, or not; but it is rather better to cook it first in a double boiler. This makes a medium sized pie. Bake thirty or forty minutes.

CORN STARCH CUSTARD PIE.
Mrs. J. A. Johnston, Emporium, Pa.

Boil three pints milk; stir into it two table-spoons corn starch wet with a little milk, and boil one minute. When nearly cold, stir in six table-spoons white sugar, the yolks of six eggs and whites of two; flavor with essence of bitter almond and pour into paste shells. Whip the remaining whites to a meringue with two table-spoons sugar and one tea-spoon vanilla. When the custard is set, draw pies to edge of oven and spread it over them quickly and brown.

CREAM PIE.
Mrs. F. R. St. John.

Beat four eggs separately. To the yolks add one cup white sugar, two cups sweet milk, and one table-spoon corn starch or flour made smooth in a little milk; flavor with lemon. Beat all well together and cook in a vessel with water around it; stir until thick like custard. Bake with one crust. Now beat one cup white sugar with the whites of the eggs and spread on top. Brown lightly in the oven. This makes two pies.

COCOANUT PIE.
Mrs. J. W. Fish.

One pint milk, one-half cocoanut, grated, one-half cup sugar, yolks of three eggs and the white of one. Beat the yolks and sugar together, then stir in the milk and cocoanut, filling the pan even full, and bake. Beat the remaining whites to a stiff froth, stirring in three table-spoons cocoanut. Pour over each pie and bake a light brown.

GREEN APPLE PIE.
Miss Lulu Browning.

Peel, core and slice tart apples enough for one pie; sprinkle over the apples about three table-spoons sugar, one tea-spoon cinnamon, one small level table-spoon sifted flour, two table-spoons water, a few bits butter; stir all together with a spoon. Put into a pie pan lined with paste, cover with a top crust and bake.

RHUBARB PIE.
Mrs. G. W. Shoemaker.

One and one-half pounds rhubarb, chopped fine, one cup raisins chopped fine, three cups brown sugar. Mix well. Put in a little butter, dredge with a little flour before putting on top crust. This makes three pies.

LEMON PIE.
Mrs. Gib. Lane.

One good sized lemon grated, one cup sugar, yolks of three eggs, small pieces butter, three table-spoons milk. Beat all together and bake in rich crust. Put a meringue of the whites with three spoons sugar on each pie, and brown lightly.

BANANA PIE.
Mrs. Wells.

Peel and slice bananas until pan is full enough, then sprinkle with sugar, two table-spoons vinegar, small piece butter, and some grated nutmeg. Bake between two crusts.

SWEET POTATO PIE.
From "The Delineator."

Stir together thoroughly one cup cooked, mashed, and strained sweet-potatoes, one pint milk, a pinch of salt, two table-spoons sugar, one tea-spoon cinnamon and two well-beaten eggs. Bake with a bottom crust only, in a quick oven, until a knife blade, when thrust in, will come out clean.

MINCE PIE.
Mrs. C. M. Childs.

Two and one-half pounds lean meat, double the quantity of apple, one and one-half pounds raisins, one pound currants, one and one-half pounds suet chopped fine, one quart cider, sugar and spices to taste. Cook slowly for an hour, then seal in jars. Put a piece of butter size of an egg in each pie.

LEMON RAISIN PIE.
Mrs. G. W. Shoemaker.

Grate the rind of one lemon, then peel off the skin and chop pulp fine; one cup seeded raisins, one cup sugar, one small cup water, and one egg well beaten. Mix all well together and bake between two crusts.

FROSTED CREAM PIE.
Mrs. U. E. Frizelle.

One pint milk, the yolks of three eggs and white of one, two table-spoons sugar, a pinch of salt. When baked, put on the frosting, made of the whites of two eggs beaten stiff, two table-spoons powdered sugar, small pinch of salt and any flavoring you choose. Set back in oven and brown.

CRUST FOR PUMPKIN PIE.
Mrs. Philip M. Gallaher.

Take pie dish and butter it well; then take some dry cornmeal and shake it around in the buttered tin; empty it out, leaving only what sticks to the tin. Have pumpkin ready the same as for any pie; pour it into tin and bake it. You will be surprised to see what a nice crust it will form.

CHOCOLATE PIE.
Mrs. J. W. Fish.

Four tea-spoons grated chocolate, one pint boiling water (let it simmer a few minutes), the yolks of two eggs and two table-spoons sugar. Mix all together like boiled custard. Make a frosting of the whites of two eggs with one tea-spoon powdered sugar.

CREAM PIE.
Mrs. J. W. Vaugun.

One cup sweet cream, three table-spoons sugar, one table-spoon flour, butter the size of an egg, a little nutmeg. Bake with one crust.

TRANSPARENT PIE.
Miss Alice Holland.

A coffee-cup not quite full of granulated sugar, one-half cup butter and cream together, three eggs beaten separately and each stiff; put the yolks in first and stir; add whites of the eggs last; flavor. Bake with under crust only. This will make two pies.

LEMON MINCE PIE.
Mrs. C. H. Sabin.

One pound raisins, two lemons, three cups sugar, six eggs, butter half the size of an egg, two cups milk. This makes four pies.

PEACH PIE.
Mrs. Frank McCormick.

Bake under crust; then fill with peaches from can; then cover peaches with a boiled custard made of two eggs and one tea-cup of milk. Keep whites of eggs to whip and cover over top of custard.

CUSTARD PIE.
Mrs. H. W. Rowley.

Beat three eggs thoroughly and add one-half cup sugar, pinch of salt and nutmeg. Pour over this nearly one quart boiling milk. Bake in hot oven, but do not let boil.

FILLING FOR LEMON PIE.
Miss Martha Shoemaker.

Take grated rind and juice of two large lemons, small cup water, one cup sugar, small piece butter, yolks of two eggs; heat until it boils, then thicken with three table-spoons flour. Bake crust first, then put in filling and bake five minutes. Put a meringue of whites of eggs beaten stiff with table-spoon sugar and a little vanilla on top; brown in oven.

MOLASSES LEMON PIE.
Mrs. Love Dill, Brooklyn, N. Y.

Three lemons, one cup sugar, one cup molasses, one and one-half cups hot water, three tea-spoons flour made smooth with melted butter, then add other ingredients. Boil two minutes and bake in crusts.

APPLE MERINGUE PIE.
From "The Ladies' Home Journal."

Pare, slice thin and stew, juicy apples, with about one tea-cup cold water in bottom of kettle to prevent burning. Cover pie plates with rich paste, fill with apples, leaving one-fourth inch at top. Bake until paste is brown, then fill with meringue made from whites of two eggs and one light table-spoon sugar. Return to oven and brown. Serve cold.

ORANGE PIE.
Mrs. Love Dill, Brooklyn, N. Y.

Three eggs, three-fourths cup white sugar, two table-spoons butter, juice and rind of one orange and one-half of a lemon.

CAKE.
LAYER.

BOILED FROSTING.
Mrs. J. E. Free.

One cup white sugar with a little cold water (boil without stirring, until it becomes a trifle brittle when put into cold water); pour this into the beaten white of an egg, with whatever flavor you choose, and beat until cold; spread on the cake. A little tartaric acid makes the icing more firm.

JELLY CAKE.
Mrs. Love Dill, Brooklyn, N. Y.

One-fourth cup butter, one and one-half cups flour, one tea-spoon soda, two tea-spoons cream tartar, three eggs, one-half cup milk, one cup sugar. Bake in layers and spread with jelly.

WHITE MOUNTAIN CAKE.
Mrs. L. M. Birely.

One cup sugar, one egg, butter size of an egg, a little salt and extract of lemon. Beat this to a cream, add one cup sweet milk, and two cups flour, into which two tea-spoons baking powder has been mixed. Bake in four layers.

FILLING.—One tea-cup thick sweet cream, whipped with two table-spoons sugar and one-half tea-spoon lemon extract.

SILVER, OR DELICATE CAKE.
Miss Lulu Browning.

Whites of six eggs, one cup sweet milk, two cups sugar, four cups sifted flour, two-thirds cup butter, flavoring and two tea-spoons baking powder. Cream the butter and sugar, then add milk, flavoring, and part of flour, beaten whites of eggs, then rest of flour. Bake in two tins lined with buttered white paper.

ICE-CREAM CAKE.
Mrs. George Comfort.

One cup sugar, one-half cup each of butter and milk, whites of three eggs, two cups flour, one and one-half tea-spoons baking powder, one tea-spoon vanilla.

FILLING.—Yolks of three eggs, one cup pulverized sugar, one and one-half tea-spoons vanilla. Beat fifteen minutes, when it will be nice and creamy. Spread between layers and on top, and set in oven a minute to harden frosting.

GOLD CAKE.

After beating to a cream one and one-half cups butter and two cups sugar, stir in the well-beaten yolks of one dozen eggs, four cups sifted flour, one tea-spoon baking powder. Bake in buttered tins one hour.

MINNEHAHA CAKE.
Mrs. I. D. O'Donnell.

One cup sugar, one-half cup each of butter and sweet milk, two tea-spoons baking powder, two cups flour, whites of four eggs.

FILLING.—One cup sugar, a little water; boil until brittle. Beat into it the whites of two eggs well beaten, and one cup seeded raisins, chopped fine.

WHITE LAYER CAKE.
Miss Alice Holland.

Whites of seven eggs beaten to stiff froth, two cups powdered sugar, one small cup butter. Cream the butter and sugar together, add one-half cup milk, three cups flour, three tea-spoons baking powder; flavor. Bake in layers, and put any kind of filling between them.

MY FAVORITE CAKE.
Mrs. E. H. Lee.

One cup butter, two cups powdered sugar, one cup sweet milk, three scant cups flour, one-half cup corn starch, four eggs, two tea-spoons each of baking powder and lemon extract. Sift the flour and sugar; whip the eggs separately, and add the whites last. Beat the butter and sugar to a cream.

FILLING.—Two-thirds cup sugar, three table-spoons hot water; boil briskly until it begins to candy, then pour over it the white of one egg beaten to a stiff froth, beating quickly all the time until cool. Spread on the cake.

PRINCE OF WALES CAKE.
Mrs. W. E. Barker.

DARK PART.—One cup brown sugar, one-half cup each of butter and sour milk, two cups flour, one cup raisins, one tea-spoon soda dissolved in warm water, one table-spoon molasses, yolks of three eggs, one table-spoon each of cinnamon and nutmeg, one-half table-spoon cloves.

LIGHT PART.—One cup flour, one-half cup each of corn starch, sweet milk and butter, one cup sugar, one large tea-spoon yeast powder, whites of three eggs. Bake in layers, and put together with icing.

RAISIN LAYER CAKE.
Mrs. L. F. Fields.

One-half cup butter, one cup each of sugar and milk, three eggs,—leaving out the white of one—two and one-half cups flour, two tea-spoons baking powder.

FILLING.—One cup sugar, four table-spoons water, boil to a syrup. Have the white of one egg beaten to a stiff froth; pour on the boiling syrup, stirring all the time; to this add one-half cup raisins, seeded and chopped fine, and one-half cup hickory nuts, chopped fine. Spread between layers and on top.

CHOCOLATE CAKE.
Miss Martha Shoemaker.

One cup sugar, one-half cup butter, two eggs, two cups flour, one-half cup milk, two tea-spoons baking powder. Mix one-half cake chocolate with one-half cup sweet milk, yolk of one egg and one cup sugar. Cook this until soft, and add to first part of recipe. Stir well together and bake in two layers. Put these together with boiled frosting flavored with vanilla. Bake in square tins.

WHITE FRUIT CAKE.
Mrs. C. M. Childs.

Take one-half of the recipe for angel food, and make two white layers; then take one-half of fruit cake recipe for one layer. Put the dark layer between the two white ones. To the boiled frosting, add one cup seeded raisins chopped fine; spread between layers and on top.

GENTLEMAN'S JELLY CAKE.
Mrs. Lovett.

Seven eggs beaten separately, two cups white sugar, one and one-half cups butter, two table-spoons water, two cups flour, two tea-spoons baking powder, a little salt.

JELLY.—Take one egg, one cup sugar, three grated apples, one lemon. Stir until it boils, then cool before putting on the cake.

ORANGE CAKE.
Mrs. G. W. Shoemaker.

Beat whites of three eggs and yolks of five, separately; cream two cups sugar and one-half cup butter; add one-half cup cold water, two and one-half cups flour, two tea-spoons baking powder, juice and grated rind of one orange, saving a table-spoon of juice for the frosting.

FILLING.—Whites of two eggs, two cups sugar, and the table-spoon of orange juice.

CREAM CAKE.
Mrs. F. R. St. John.

Two cups powdered sugar, two-thirds cup butter, one-half cup milk, three cups flour, four eggs, one and one-half tea-spoons baking powder. Bake in layers and spread with the

FILLING.—One-half pint milk, two small tea-spoons corn starch, one egg, one tea-spoon vanilla, one-half cup sugar. Heat the milk to boiling, and stir in the corn starch wet with a little cold milk; take out a little and mix with the beaten egg and sugar, and then return it to the rest of the custard and boil, stirring constantly until thick; let it cool before adding the vanilla.

MAPLE CAKE.
Miss Maggie Peck.

Whites of seven eggs, one cup butter, one and one-half cups sugar, one-half cup sweet milk, one tea-spoon baking powder; flour.

FILLING.—One cup maple syrup, one tea-spoon sugar; boil until it becomes brittle. Pour the boiling syrup into beaten whites of two eggs; beat stiff and pour over the cake.

VARIETY CAKE.
Mrs. J. F. Sleeper.

Four eggs, one-half cup butter, two cups sugar, one cup milk, three cups flour. Take half of the recipe and put some spice, molasses and fruit in it. Put the layers together with icing.

COCOANUT CAKE.
Mrs. Gib. Lane.

To the well-beaten yolks of six eggs, add two cups powdered sugar, three-fourths cup butter, one cup sweet milk, three and one-half cups flour, one level table-spoon soda and two of cream tartar. Whites of four eggs well beaten. Bake in jelly tins.

ICING.—Grate one cocoanut, beat the whites of four eggs and add one tea-cup powdered sugar; mix thoroughly with the grated cocoanut, and spread evenly on the layers when cold.

GOLDEN CREAM CAKE.
Mrs. W. H. Donovan.

Cream one cup sugar and one-fourth cup butter; add one-half cup sweet milk, the well-beaten whites of three eggs, one and one-half cups flour, one-half tea-spoon soda and one tea-spoon cream tartar sifted with the flour; bake in three deep jelly tins. Beat very light the yolks of two eggs, one cup sugar, and two table-spoons rich sweet cream. Flavor with vanilla and spread on cakes.

RIBBON CAKE.
Mrs. Andrew Campbell.

Two cups sugar, one cup each of butter and milk, four scant cups flour, four eggs, one-half tea-spoon soda, one tea-spoon cream tartar. Beat butter and sugar to a cream and flavor; add eggs and milk, mix soda and cream tartar with flour, and beat quickly. Put two-thirds of the mixture in two tins and bake; to the other one-third add four tea-spoons cinnamon, one cup currants, one-eighth pound citron, cut fine. Bake this in one tin. Spread jelly or frosting between layers.

PITTSBURGH CAKE.
Mrs. J. W. Vaughn.

Two cups sugar, yolks of three eggs, one cup sweet milk, one table-spoon butter, two tea-spoons baking powder.

Frosting.—Take whites of three eggs and three-fourths pound pulverized sugar.

MAUD S. CAKE.
Mrs. J. F. Melcher, Walla-Walla, Wash.

Two cups each of sugar and butter whipped to a cream; whites of five eggs, one cup milk, two and one-half cups flour, two tea-spoons baking powder. Sift the flour three times, then put in the baking powder, and sift twice more. Grate three table-spoons of Baker's chocolate, add a little sugar and dissolve in hot milk; then add three table-spoons cake dough in layer pans, and drop the chocolate dough through them. Put the cake together with cocoanut, flavor with vanilla.

CREAM CAKE.
Mrs. H. F. Clement.

Three eggs, one cup each of sugar and flour, one tea-spoon baking powder, one-half cup sweet cream. Bake in jelly tins.

Filling.—Whip one-half cup thick sweet cream, sweeten and flavor. Spread between the layers and on top.

LEMON CAKE.
Miss Jennie Kimball.

Three cups sugar, one cup butter, four eggs, one cup sweet milk, one and one-half tea-spoons baking powder, one tea-spoon lemon extract. Cream the butter and sugar; add the well-beaten yolks of the eggs, then the flour with the baking powder sifted into it, then the milk, and lastly the essence. Bake in two layers. Beat stiff the remaining whites, add the juice of one small lemon, and enough powdered sugar to make a stiff icing. Spread between the layers.

FIG CAKE.
Mrs. O. F. Goddard.

One cup sugar, one-half cup each of butter and milk, three eggs, two cups flour, one tea-spoon baking powder. Boil two cups figs until tender, then sweeten, chop fine and spread between the layers, and ice the top.

BANANA CAKE.
Mrs. Charles Spear.

Five eggs, one and one-half cups sugar, one cup butter, one-half cup sweet milk, two cups flour sifted three times, one level tea-spoon baking powder. Bake in layers.

FILLING.—Whip one-half pint cream, three table-spoons sugar; chop six bananas and beat in the cream. Spread between the layers.

FRENCH CHOCOLATE CAKE.
Mrs. J. E. Free.

The whites of seven eggs, two cups sugar, two-thirds cup butter, one cup milk, three cups flour, three tea-spoons baking powder. The chocolate part of the cake is made just the same, only use the yolks of the eggs with a cup of grated chocolate stirred into it. Bake in layers alternating light and dark, then spread a custard between them, or boiled icing if preferred.

CHOCOLATE ICING.
From "The Ladies' Home Journal."

Two cups sugar, and just enough water to moisten; boil until clear. Add two cakes grated chocolate and one egg beaten stiff; flavor with vanilla and beat until cold. After covering a cake with chocolate icing, shell a cup of English walnuts and arrange over the top in circles. Daisies may be made by placing one with seven around it, at intervals over the cake. Raisins may be iced and dried in the oven, then placed upon the chocolate if so desired.

COCOANUT CAKE.
Mrs. Love Dill, Brooklyn, N. Y.

Four cups flour, three cups sugar, one cup milk, five eggs beaten separately (reserve the whites of three for icing), one cup butter, two tea-spoons cream tartar, one tea spoon soda, one-half cocoanut grated and put into the cake; the other one-half put with the whites of three eggs, and one-half cup powdered sugar, with a little orange water or lemon juice for the icing. Bake in jelly tins, and spread the icing between layers and on top; set in the oven a few minutes.

WHITE FRUIT CAKE.
Mrs. W. A. Allen.

To one cup butter beaten to a cream, add two cups sugar, three cups flour in which two tea-spoons baking powder have been mixed, and the stiffly beaten whites of six eggs. Bake in jelly tins. When done, and while still hot, put between the layers this

FILLING.—Chop fine one-fourth pound each of figs, preserved ginger, seeded raisins, citron, blanched almonds, and stir them into the well-beaten whites of three eggs, one cup powdered sugar and the juice of one lemon. Frost the whole quickly.

HAZEL-NUT CAKE.
Mrs. I. D. O'Donnell.

One cup sugar, one egg and yolks of two, one-fourth cup butter stirred to a cream, two-thirds cup milk, two cups flour, two tea-spoons baking powder. Bake in layers.

FILLING.—One cup each of sugar and thick cream, one cup hazel nuts chopped. Boil until like taffy, then spread between the layers.

ICE-CREAM CAKE.
Mrs. J. A. Johnston, Emporium, Pa.

One cup butter, two cups sugar, one cup milk, whites of five eggs, three tea-spoons baking powder. Bake in layers.

FILLING.—Three small cups sugar dissolved in a little water and boiled to a thick syrup; cool a little, and pour over the unbeaten whites of three eggs. Beat together one-half hour, and spread between the layers.

FROSTED CREAMS.
Mrs. W. B. Chrysler.

Four eggs (reserve the whites of two for frosting), one and one half cups each of molasses and sugar, one cup shortening, two and one-half tea-spoons ginger, two tea-spoons soda, one cup water, spices to taste. Roll into oblong pieces, bake, and frost the top.

MOLASSES LAYER CAKE.
Mrs. G. W. Shoemaker.

One-half cup each of sugar and molasses, two-thirds cup hot water, one and one-half cups flour, butter size of an egg, one egg, one tea-spoon each of soda, vanilla and lemon extracts.

FILLING.—One-half pint milk, one egg, one tea-spoon corn starch, one-half cup sugar. Flavor.

GELATINE FROSTING.
Mrs. Love Dill, Booklyn, N. Y.

One tea-spoon gelatine, two table-spoons cold water; when the gelatine is soft, add one table-spoon hot water. When entirely dissolved, add one cup powdered sugar, and beat while yet warm, until white and light; lemon to taste. This frosts one sheet of cake.

⊷LOAF.⊶

ANGEL FOOD.
Mrs. J. E. Free.

Put into tumbler of flour, one tea-spoon cream tartar, then sift five times; also sift one and one-half glasses white powdered sugar. Beat to a stiff froth the whites of eleven eggs; stir the sugar into the eggs by degrees, very lightly and carefully, adding three tea-spoons vanilla. After this, add the flour, stirring quickly and lightly; pour it into a clean tin cake dish which should not be buttered or lined. Bake in moderate oven forty-five minutes. You can make a layer cake of this by pouring the above into two cake tins, and spread whipped cream between layers and on top. This makes a very nice cake.

SIX EGG CAKE.
Mrs. E. S. Holmes.

Six eggs, one cup butter, two cups sugar, one-half cup milk, three and one-half cups flour, two tea-spoons cream tartar, one-half tea-spoon soda; flavor.

NUT CAKE.
Mrs. J. R. Goss.

One-half cup granulated sugar, two heaping cups flour, three-fourths cup sweet milk, one-half cup butter, whites of five eggs, one cup nut meats, two full tea-spoons baking powder.

CORN STARCH CAKE.
Mrs. G. W. Shoemaker.

One cup sugar, one-half cup each of butter and milk, whites of three eggs, one cup flour, one-half cup corn starch, one heaping tea-spoon baking powder.

HICKORY-NUT CAKE.
Mrs. W. A. Allen.

One cup butter, four eggs, two cups sugar, one-half cup milk, two cups flour, one cup each of chopped raisins and hickorynuts, one-half tea-spoon soda, juice of one-half lemon.

WHIPPED CREAM CAKE.
Mrs. R. T. Allen.

One cup sugar, two eggs, two table-spoons softened butter, four table-spoons milk. Beat all well together, and add one cup flour in which two tea-spoons baking powder has been mixed. Bake in rather small square dripping pan. When cake is cool, spread with whipped cream, and serve while fresh.

CREAM SPONGE CAKE.
Mrs. U. E. Frizelle.

Put into a bowl one large cup flour, into which one tea-spoon cream tartar has been sifted; one cup powdered sugar, a little salt. Then break into the cup that the flour and sugar were measured in, two eggs, beat two minutes, then fill the cup with sweet cream, add this to flour and sugar in bowl; also one-half tea-spoon soda, dissolved in one table-spoon hot water. Beat well, bake quickly and ice top.

WALNUT CAKE.
Mrs. C. M. Childs.

Whites of three eggs beaten to stiff froth, one tea-cup even full sugar, one-half cup butter, one tea-cup sweet milk, two and one-half cups flour—light measure. Beat butter and sugar to a cream, add milk and one tea-spoon salt, then flour; flavor to taste. Add two pounds walnuts chopped fine; add eggs last.

CITRON CAKE.
Mrs. J. A. Johnston, Emporium, Pa.

One cup butter, two and one-half cups sugar, one cup sweet milk, four cups flour, whites of nine eggs, two heaping tea-spoons baking powder. Mix butter and sugar together thoroughly, stir in milk slowly, add beaten whites of eggs, then flour and baking powder; flavor with vanilla. Put into cake tins a layer of cake, then a layer of citron cut into thin slices. Alternate in this way, until all the cake sponge is used.

PORK CAKE.
Mrs. Fred Mashaw.

Three and one-half cups fresh pork chopped fine, two cups sour milk, two and one-half cups molasses, six cups brown sugar, two table-spoons each of ground cloves, cinnamon and allspice, fifty cents worth each of seedless raisins and currants, four tea-spoons soda, one tea-spoon salt, nine eggs, one-half slice citron if you like, and flour to make rather stiff. Bake each loaf in slow oven four or five hours.

LADY'S CAKE.
Mrs. S. F. Mills.

One-half cup butter, one and one-half cups sugar, two cups flour, nearly one cup sweet milk, one-half tea-spoon soda, one tea-spoon cream tartar, whites of four eggs well beaten; flavor with peach or almond.

A CAKE WITHOUT BUTTER.
Mrs. A. Hirsch.

Beat well five eggs, to which add six ounces of flour; flavor with bitter almond, and if you like, add thin slices of citron. Bake in mould in moderate oven.

CORN STARCH PUFFS.
Miss Martha Shoemaker.

One cup sugar, one-half cup butter, one cup corn starch, four eggs, two tea-spoons baking powder, flavor with vanilla, and bake in gem tins. Frost them when nearly cold.

MARBLE CAKE.
Miss Mattie Murphy.

WHITE PART.—Whites of four eggs, one cup white sugar, one-half cup butter, one-half cup sweet milk, two tea-spoons baking powder, one tea-spoon lemon or vanilla, two and one-half cups sifted flour.

DARK PART.—Yolks of four eggs, one cup brown sugar, one-half cup cooking molasses, one-half cup sour milk, one tea-spoon each of ground cloves, cinnamon and mace, one nutmeg grated, one tea-spoon soda dissolved in a little sour milk, and add after part of flour is stirred in, one and one-half cups sifted flour. Drop one spoon at a time of each kind into a well buttered cake dish, until all the sponge is used. Drop so the cake will be streaked to resemble marble.

WHITE PUFF CAKE.
Miss Martha Shoemaker.

Two cups sugar, one cup each of butter and milk, one pint sifted flour, three tea-spoons baking powder. Flavor with almonds, and bake in dripping pan. Put on a thick boiled frosting, and cut into squares.

DELICATE CAKE.
Mrs. E. S. Holmes.

Whites of four eggs, one cup sweet milk (running over), two cups confectioner's sugar, one-half cup butter, two and one-half cups flour, one heaping tea-spoon baking powder.

MARBLE CHOCOLATE CAKE.
Miss Lulu Browning.

One-half cup each of butter and milk, two cups flour, one egg, one tea-spoon baking powder. Have ready five tea-spoons grated chocolate moistened with vanilla. Stir in a cup of the cake mixture, and put in alternate layers. Frost first with white, then with chocolate.

FRUIT CAKE.
Mrs. H. D. Claflin.

One cup each of sweet milk and brown sugar, one-half cup butter, three cups flour, one-half pound raisins, one cup currants, one salt-spoon ground cloves, one tea-spoon cinnamon, one nutmeg grated, two eggs, two tea-spoons baking powder, one tea-spoon allspice.

BRIDE'S CAKE.
Mrs. W. F. Leroy.

The whites of twelve eggs, three cups sugar, one small cup butter, one cup sweet milk, four small cups flour, one-half cup corn starch, two tea-spoons baking powder, lemon to taste.

COFFEE CAKE.
Mrs. W. E. Barker.

One cup each of sugar, molasses and cold coffee, two-thirds cup butter, two eggs, four cups flour, one tea-spoon soda, one cup raisins, one and one-half cups currants, one tea-spoon nutmeg.

MOTHER'S FRUIT CAKE.
Mrs. Paul McCormick.

Five eggs, one tea-cup butter, two tea-cups sugar, three tea-cups flour, one tea-cup each of raisins, currants and milk, one tea-spoon soda, two tea-spoons cream tartar, and all kinds of spices.

JELLY ROLL.
Mrs. Wells.

One cup each of sugar and flour, four eggs, four table-spoons water, a little salt. Bake in large bread pan, and when done spread with jelly and roll in damp cloth.

COFFEE CAKE.
Miss Bertha Crowe.

One cup butter, two cups sugar, four eggs, one tea-spoon soda, one large cup strong coffee, two cups each of raisins and currants, two tea-spoons cinnamon, one tea-spoon each of cloves and allspice. Thicken with flour like fruit cake.

SPONGE CAKE.
Mrs. Paul McCormick.

One cup each of sifted sugar and flour, and one level tea-spoon baking powder, all sifted together. Make a hollow in the center, and break four eggs into it, also four table-spoons water, and one tea-spoon vanilla extract. Stir all together quickly, and bake in moderate oven. This recipe baked in two layers, with whipped cream between and on top, is very nice.

DOLLY VARDEN CAKE.
Mrs. B. W. Toole.

WHITE PART.—One cup sugar, one-half cup each of butter and milk, one and one-half cups flour, one tea-spoon yeast powder, whites of three eggs.

DARK PART.—One-half cup each of molasses, sugar and coffee, one tea-spoon soda, yolks of three eggs, one cup each of raisins and currants, one-fourth pound citron, one-half cup butter; spices to taste.

CREAM PUFFS.
Mrs. F. B. Conolly.

Boil with one large cup water, one-half tea-cup butter. Stir into this while boiling, one tea-cup flour. Let cool, then stir in four eggs, one at a time, without beating. Drop on tins and bake in fairly hot oven.

CREAM.—Beat together three table-spoons flour, one egg, one-third cup sugar. Stir into it one-half pint milk while boiling; flavor with vanilla.

SUNSHINE CAKE.
Mrs. J. W. Fish.

Whites of eleven eggs, yolks of six, one and one-half tea-cups granulated sugar, (measured after one sifting,) one tea-cup flour, (measured after one sifting,) one tea-spoon flavoring. Beat whites of eggs to stiff froth, and stir in gradually, first the cream tartar, then the sugar; beat the yolks and add to them the whites, sugar and flavoring; finally stir in flour. Mix quickly and well. Bake in slow oven, in angel cake tins.

POUND CAKE.
Mrs. Barth.

One pound each of butter and powdered sugar, one dozen eggs beaten separately, four pounds flour; cream butter and sugar together with your hand, add yolks, then whites of eggs. Take wooden spoon and beat well; add flour last, with tea-spoon baking powder; flavor with vanilla.

NEW YEAR'S MARBLE CAKE.
Miss Ruth Mills.

WHITE PART.—Whites of four eggs, one cup white sugar, one-half cup each of butter and sweet milk, two tea-spoons baking powder, one tea-spoon vanilla, and two and one-half cups flour.

DARK PART.—Yolks of four eggs, one cup brown sugar, one-half cup each of molasses, butter and sour milk, one tea-spoon each of cloves, cinnamon, mace, soda and nutmeg, one and one-half cups sifted flour. Put into the cake dish alternately, first light part and then dark.

CUP CAKE.
Miss Maggie Botkin.

Five eggs, three cups sugar, one cup each of milk, butter and flour, one-half tea-spoon soda. Bake in slow oven half an hour.

WHITE CAKE.
Mrs. S. R. Salsbury.

One cup butter, two cups sugar, one cup sweet milk, three cups flour, whites of five eggs well beaten, two tea-spoons baking powder. To use this for marble cake, take the yolks of the eggs, follow same rule, add one-half tea-spoon cloves, and one tea-spoon cinnamon. Be sure to stir the cake to equal thickness in the batter.

BOSTON CREAM PUFFS.
Mrs. W. H. Donovan.

Put one-half pint hot water and two-thirds cup butter over the fire; when boiling stir in one and one-half cups flour, and continue stirring until smooth and the mixture leaves the sides of the sauce-pan; remove from the fire, cool, and beat into it five well-beaten eggs. Drop on warm greased tins, one table-spoon in a place, leaving space between to prevent touching; brush over with the white of an egg, and bake ten or fifteen minutes in quick oven. When the cakes are done they will be hollow. When cold slice off the top, fill space with cream and replace top.

CREAM.—Take one pint milk, place one-half in a tin pail and set in boiling water; reserve from the other one-half, two table-spoons to mix with the eggs, and into the rest while cold, mix one cup flour until smooth. When the milk is hot, stir in the flour and let it boil thicker than boiled custard; then beat two eggs with the two table-spoons milk, one cup granulated sugar, a level tea-spoon butter, and one tea-spoon vanilla or lemon. Continue stirring until it is so thick it will drop from the spoon when cold, and not pour from it.

PLAIN CAKE.
Mrs. C. H. Sabin.

Break two eggs into a tea-cup, and fill it with thick sour cream; one cup sugar, one and one-half cups flour, one-half tea-spoon each of soda and salt; flavor with vanilla.

SNOW CAKE.
Miss Ella Mills.

One-half tea-cup butter, one tea-cup sugar, one and one-half tea-cups flour, one-half cup sweet milk, whites of four eggs, one tea-spoon baking powder; flavor with lemon.

FRUIT CAKE.
Mrs. R. K. Babcock.

One and one-half cups molasses, one cup each of sugar and sour milk, one tea-spoon soda, two tea-spoons ginger, one tea-spoon each of cinnamon and nutmeg, one and one-half cups each of raisins and currants, one-half cup each of citron and butter, flour enough to stiffen. Bake two hours.

SPICE CAKE.
Mrs. G. C. Stull.

Three eggs, two cups sugar, three cups flour, one-half cup butter, one cup sour cream, one tea-spoon soda, two tea-spoons each of cloves, ginger, allspice and cinnamon.

APPLE CAKE.
Mrs. W. F. Leroy.

Soak two cups dried apples over night. In the morning drain and chop fine; add one cup molasses and let it boil slowly on back of stove three or four hours, and add one and one-half cups brown sugar, one cup butter, one-half cup sour milk, one tea-spoon each of cloves, allspice, cinnamon and soda, three eggs, three and one-half cups flour. Bake in two square tins or one five quart basin; if in the latter, bake two hours.

SIX MONTHS CAKE.
Miss Martha Shoemaker.

Four eggs, four cups flour, one pound raisins, two cups sugar, one cup molasses, one and one-half pounds butter, one cup milk, one tea-spoon soda, and two tea-spoons all kinds of spices.

COOKIES, CRULLERS, ETC.

CHOICE COOKIES.
Mrs. J. F. Sleeper.

Two eggs, two cups sugar, one cup butter, one-third cup sweet milk, two tea-spoons cream tartar, one tea-spoon soda, one-half tea-spoon nutmeg; flour.

GINGER COOKIES.
Mrs. R. R. Crowe.

One cup each of sugar and butter, three eggs, one cup sour milk, one tea-spoon soda, one cup molasses, one table-spoon ginger; flour.

SOFT GINGER BREAD.
Mrs. W. E. Barker.

One cup each of sorghum, sugar and lard, one table-spoon each of ginger and cinnamon, one cup sour milk, one tea-spoon soda, two eggs, and enough flour to stiffen.

DOUGHNUTS.
Mrs. F. R. St. John.

One egg, one cup each of sugar and sour milk, one tea-spoon soda in the milk, butter size of a hickory-nut, a little each of salt and nutmeg, two tea-spoons baking powder in the flour. Fry brown and roll in powdered sugar when nearly cold.

NO MATTER CAKE.
Mrs. C. H. Sabin.

The whites of one egg beaten to a stiff froth, pinch of salt, and enough flour to roll thin. Cut with any kind of cake cutter, fry in hot lard, and immediately sprinkle with sugar.

LANCASTER COUNTY GINGER BREAD.
Mrs. J. F. Sleeper.

One pint each of molasses and buttermilk, butter size of an egg, one table-spoon each of ginger, cloves and soda, a little salt and three pints of flour.

GINGER COOKIES.
Miss Lulu Browning.

One pint syrup, one cup each of sugar and lard, one and one-half cups sour milk, one-half ounce ginger, a rounding tea-spoon soda, one-half tea-spoon salt. Mix with flour until stiff, then roll thin.

COOKIES.
Mrs. F. B. Conolly.
One cup butter, two cups sugar, five table-spoons milk, two eggs, one tea-spoon cinnamon, three tea-spoons baking powder. Do not make too stiff.

GINGER PUFFS.
Mrs. M. J. Crampton.
Mix together one cup each of sugar, molasses and cold water, one-half cup shortening, five cups flour, one tea-spoon each of ginger and saleratus, one tea-spoon cloves or cinnamon, a little salt. After ingredients are well mixed, drop from a spoon portions of the dough as large as an egg upon greased pans, one inch apart. Bake in quick oven.

SOFT GINGER BREAD.
Mrs. H. M. Allen.
One cup each of molasses and brown sugar, one-half cup butter or lard, one cup milk, three and one-half cups flour, two eggs, one tea-spoon ginger, two tea-spoons baking powder. Put molasses, lard, sugar and ginger on the stove and let come to a boil, and when cool, add eggs and other ingredients.

GINGER SNAPS.
Mrs. G. C. Stull.
One cup sugar, two cups molasses, one cup butter and lard mixed, one table-spoon ginger, one cup boiling water, two tea-spoons soda, pinch of salt. Mix sugar and butter first, then add other ingredients.

CHOCOLATE GINGER BREAD.
Maria Parloa.
Mix in a large bowl one cup molasses, one-half cup sour milk or cream, one tea-spoon each of ginger and cinnamon, one-half tea-spoon salt. Dissolve one tea-spoon soda in a little cold water; add this and two table-spoons melted butter to mixture. Then stir in two cups sifted flour, and finally add two ounces Baker's chocolate and one table-spoon butter melted together. Pour mixture into three well buttered deep tin plates, and bake in moderate oven twenty minutes.

DOUGHNUTS.
Mrs. Henry Terrell.
Three eggs, one table-spoon melted butter, one cup sour milk, one-half cup sugar, one tea-spoon soda. Flavor to taste. Mix stiffer than for cake. Drop from a spoon into hot lard.

SUGAR COOKIES.
Mrs. H. M. Allen.

One cup each of sugar, butter and sour milk, one tea-spoon soda. Mix soft; roll thin with sugar on top.

CHOCOLATE WAFERS.
Maria Parloa.

Grate four ounces W. Baker's chocolate and mix with it two table-spoons flour and one-fourth tea-spoon each of cloves, cinnamon and baking powder. Separate six eggs. Add one cup powdered sugar to the yolks and beat until very light; then add juice and grated rind of one lemon, and beat five minutes. Then add the dry mixture, and with a spoon, lightly cut in the whites. Pour mixture into buttered shallow pans about one-half inch thick. Bake in a moderate oven one hour. When cool, spread a thin layer of currant jelly over one sheet, and place the other on top. Use vanilla icing, and when it hardens, cut into squares. Particularly nice with ice cream.

CRULLERS.
Mrs. M. J. Crampton.

Two cups sugar, two eggs, one and one-half cups water, butter size of an egg. Flavor to taste. Mix stiff enough to roll.

DOUGHNUTS.
Mrs. R. R. Crowe.

Two cups sugar, one table-spoon butter, three eggs well beaten, one and one-half cups milk, one-half nutmeg, four tea-spoons baking powder; flour stiff enough to roll.

COCOANUT DROPS.
From "Parlor and Kitchen."

Two cups cocoanut, one cup sugar, one table-spoon flour, white of one egg beaten stiff. Drop on buttered paper and sift sugar over them. Bake fifteen minutes.

RING JUMBLES.
Marion Harland.

Three-fourths pound butter, one pound sugar, four eggs, one pound flour, small wine glass rose water. Cream the butter and sugar, add yolks, then rose water, next one-half the flour; lastly the whites stirred in the remaining flour. Line a shallow pan with greased paper, and with a table-spoon of dough form regular rings, leaving a hole in the center of each. Bake quickly and sift sugar over them. Can substitute lemon or vanilla for rose water.

SOFT GINGER BREAD.
Mrs. H. W. Rowley.

One egg, one cup molasses, one-half cup melted butter, one tea-spoon each of soda and ginger; stir in two cups flour, and one cup cold water last. Bake slowly.

MERINGUE KISSES.
Mrs. Love Dill, Brooklyn, N. Y.

Beat whites of four eggs until very stiff, beat in gradually one pound powdered sugar, one tea-spoon at a time, eight drops essence of lemon, beating the whole very hard; lay a sheet of wet paper on bottom of pan. Drop on a little of the meringue and jelly to taste. With a large spoon pile on the meringue over each lump of jelly. Set in a warm oven; when slightly colored, they are done. Take out, place bottoms together, lay on a sieve, and dry in a warm oven until the bottoms stick and form a ball.

GINGER SNAPS.
Mrs. Love Dill, Brooklyn, N. Y.

Two cups molasses, one cup lard, one table-spoon ginger, one table-spoon saleratus dissolved in a little hot water; flour enough to roll thin.

FRUIT.

TO PRESERVE FRUIT.
Mrs. Henry Terrell.

One ounce of salycilic acid dissolved in two gallons warm water with six pounds granulated sugar. See that all is dissolved, then add two gallons more cold water and mix well. Take sound fruit, clean well, and pack closely in jars; pour liquid over fruit until well covered, then set in cool place and it will keep until used. For preserves, sweet pickles, and apple butter, one tablespoon of the liquid to the gallon.

ORANGES FILLED WITH JELLY.
Mrs. Philip M. Gallauer.

Select large oranges, and from top of each remove with sharp knife, piece the size of a quarter of a dollar; with the handle of tea-spoon, take out pulp, being careful not to break rinds, and throw them into cold water. Press juice from pulp, strain, put juice and isinglass (allow one ounce isinglass to six oranges) over fire; stir constantly and boil four or five minutes. Color half the jelly bright rose color with red currant or cranberry jelly. Drain and wipe rinds, and when jelly is cold, fill with alternate strips of the two colored jellies. When perfectly cold cut into quarters with very sharp knife, and arrange tastefully in a glass dish. This makes a beautiful ornamental dish for the dinner table.

PLUM BUTTER.
Mrs. R. R. Crowe.

One peck plums (wild, if possible), one-half bushel sweet apples; cook apples and plums in separate vessels with small quantity of water. When soft, put them through coarse sieve, and to each pound of pulp, allow three-fourths pound sugar. Cook until thick as apple butter, perhaps two hours.

COMPOTE OF APPLES.
From "The Delineator."

Place one cup each of water and sugar in a pan. Pare and core eight or ten apples, or as many as you can easily place in the dish. Cook them in the syrup until soft, but not mashed. When cold put one spoon of jelly with each apple and serve with whipped cream.

APPLES SMOTHERED IN JELLY.
Mrs. M. J. Crampton.

Select tart, juicy apples; pare and remove cores with corer. Place them in saucepan with boiling water, half enough to cover them, putting one table-spoon white sugar into each apple. Cook until they are well done, but retain their form; remove to dish from which they will be served. To the juice, add sugar in the proportion of one-half cup to one-half pint of juice; pour jelly over them. If a few pieces of apple peel be stewed in the juice, then removed, it will give a nice color to the jelly.

GRAPE JELLY.
Mrs. Philip M. Gallaher.

Wash grapes the evening before making the jelly, to be sure they are perfectly dry before cooking them. Pick small bunches from main stem, put them in porcelain kettle and cook very soft; turn into a flannel bag to drain. To one pint of juice, add one pint sugar, and boil twenty minutes. Never jelly a larger quantity than one pint in the same vessel at the same time.

PRESERVED GREEN TOMATOES.
Mrs. F. S. Mills.

Take one lemon, one pound light brown sugar to one pound green tomatoes; grate rind of the lemon, pare off the thick part, which is not to be used; slice thinly and remove all seeds. Scald and peel the tomatoes; put water enough with the sugar to dissolve it, and when boiling, remove scum and add tomatoes. Cook slowly for two hours.

PRESERVED CITRON.
Mrs. G. W. Shoemaker.

Do not quite cover citron with water; boil one hour; strain, and use as much sugar as citron. Make a moderate syrup; put in two lemons to one pound citron; boil twenty minutes, strain, make a thick syrup, and turn it on the citron.

PRESERVED FIGS.
Mrs. Philip M. Gallaher.

Select fine, large, white figs, as nearly as possible of equal ripeness; peel and weigh them. Boil slowly until tender, but not broken; take them out with care and lay on platters. Throw away the liquor and prepare a thick syrup of sugar, as many pounds as of fruit; boil well and skim. Put in figs and cook slowly until transparent; when nearly done put in a few slices of lemon. Put in glass jars.

PRESERVED BLACKBERRIES.
Mrs. Barth.
Mash berries before preserving, using one pound sugar to one pound of berries.

PENNSYLVANIA APPLE BUTTER.
Mrs F. S. Mills.
Pare, core and quarter three barrels of nice, ripe, sweet apples. Boil down two barrels of new cider to one-half that quantity; then add apples to cider. Proceed with the boiling, keep constantly stirring. It should boil until quite thick. Add one-fourth pound ground allspice. Let cool and it is ready for jars.

CRANBERRY JELLY.
From "The Ladies' Home Journal."
Wash one quart cranberries, put them in a pan with one-half pint water and one-half pound white sugar. Boil twenty minutes, and press through strainer into a mould. When cool, this should form a perfect mould of bright crimson jelly.

PICKLES.

TO MAKE VINEGAR.
Mrs. M. J. Crampton.

To one gallon rain water, add one pint brown sugar or molasses, and one pint corn, off the cob. Put into a jar covered with cloth. Set in the sun, and in three weeks it will be good vinegar.

ANOTHER.—To one gallon water add one pound sugar, a small pint hop yeast; sponge, and let it get light as for bread; boil one pint corn until tender. When cool, pour all together into an open keg. In three weeks it will be good vinegar.

FRENCH MUSTARD.
Mrs. J. F. Sleeper.

One drachm each of ground cloves and allspice, one ounce white sugar, three ounces mustard, two ounces wheat flour. Boil in sufficient vinegar to make a paste.

CHILLI SAUCE.
Mrs. B. Woods.

Fifteen pounds ripe tomatoes peeled and chopped, one and one-half pounds brown sugar, one pint vinegar, two large onions chopped very fine, one tea-cup salt, four red peppers, one ounce each of black and white pepper, cloves, cinnamon. Cook thoroughly.

GREEN TOMATO PICKLE.
Mrs. Lovett.

Pare green tomatoes and chop very fine; add some salt. Stir thoroughly and put in a colander to drain, then cook in clear water until tender.

PICKLE.—Three pounds sugar, one pint vinegar, one pint water, if the vinegar is very strong, one ounce each of cloves and cinnamon, few green peppers. This is for seven pounds of fruit.

SWEET PEAR PICKLE.
Mrs. Philip M. Gallaher.

To one pint good vinegar, take four pounds brown sugar, one-fourth pound each of cinnamon stick and cloves. Tie the spices in small bags, and boil with sugar and vinegar until a good syrup is formed. Put in Bartlett or Sickle pears; place on back of stove. Cover closely and cook very slowly until they can be pierced through with a straw.

TOMATO CATSUP.
Mrs. R. R. Crowe.

Fifty pounds ripe tomatoes, five onions, three pints vinegar, sugar and Cayenne pepper to taste. Boil to the consistency of catsup.

WATER MELON PICKLE.
Mrs. C. M. Childs.

Pare off green part of rind, and the red at core; cut into pieces one or two inches in length, place in kettle in the proportion of one gallon rind, two heaping tea-spoons salt, and water to nearly cover. Boil until tender enough to pick into pieces with a fork; pour into colander to drain, and dry a few pieces at a time, pressing with a towel. To one quart cider vinegar, put three pints sugar; boil, skim, and pour boiling hot over the fruit, repeating each day until the fruit is the same color all through, and the syrup is like thin molasses. Put the melon into a jar, sprinkle bits (stick) cinnamon and a few cloves over it; add another layer of fruit, then spices, until the jar is full. Scald the syrup each morning for three days, and pour boiling hot over the fruit. Put in the melon and boil twenty minutes, then put into a jar and pour the syrup over it. If a scum rises, drain. Then add the melon, and boil until the syrup is thin, like molasses.

PICKLED CABBAGE.
Mrs. J. A. Johnston, Emporium, Pa.

Halve and quarter twenty-five small heads cabbage, lay them in a wooden tray; sprinkle thickly with salt, and set in the cellar until next day. Drain and wipe dry, lay in the sun for two hours, cover with cold vinegar for twelve hours; season with equal parts of mace, cloves and whole white peppers, one cup sugar to every gallon vinegar, and one tea-spoon celery seed for every pint. Pack the cabbage in a stone jar; boil the vinegar and spices five minutes, and pour on the cabbage hot. Set away in cool, dry place for six weeks.

CHOPPED PICKLES.
Mrs. W. B. Chrysler.

One-half bushel green tomatoes chopped fine, one dozen each of onions and peppers; sprinkle over with one pint salt, and let stand over night. In the morning, cover with vinegar and cook slowly one hour; drain again and add two pounds sugar, two table-spoons each of cinnamon and cloves. Cover with cold vinegar.

CHIPPED PEARS.
Mrs. G. W. Shoemaker.

Ten pounds pears, eight pounds sugar, three lemons—grate and put in the juice. Pare the pears and chip as you would potatoes. Put all together and clear, then can them hot.

CHILLI SAUCE.
Mrs. R. R. Crowe.

Fifty pounds ripe tomatoes, sixteen onions, two quarts vinegar, one tea-spoon cinnamon; sugar and red pepper to taste.

MIXED PICKLES.
Mrs. R. T. Allen.

Three hundred small cucumbers, four large green peppers sliced fine, two large heads cauliflower, three heads white cabbage shredded fine, nine large onions sliced, one quart small string beans cut into inch pieces, one quart small green tomatoes sliced. Put all in a strong brine for twenty-four hours, drain three hours, then sprinkle in one-fourth pound each of black and white mustard seed, one table-spoon black pepper. Let the whole come to a boil in just enough vinegar to cover, with a little alum put in. Drain, and when cold, mix one pint ground mustard and put in. Cover the whole with good cider vinegar.

SPICED TOMATOES.
Mrs. Philip M. Gallaher.

For seven pounds tomatoes, take three and one-half pounds sugar, one pint strong vinegar, one table-spoon whole cloves, and three sticks cinnamon. Boil thirty-five minutes; put sugar and vinegar on to boil; remove skins from tomatoes and drop in.

SOUR TOMATOES.
Mrs. S. R. Miller.

One-half dozen large cucumbers, one-half ounce each of black and white pepper, three pods red peppers; peel and split the cucumbers (scrape out seeds), sprinkle a little salt on them and let stand for two hours. Dry them with a cloth. Boil together vinegar and pepper and pour boiling hot over the cucumbers.

FRENCH PICKLES.
Mrs. R. T. Hanna.

Fifteen pounds green tomatoes sliced, six large onions sliced; throw over these one tea-cup salt and let stand over night. In the morning drain thoroughly, scald fifteen minutes in one quart vinegar and two quarts water; drain, then take four quarts vinegar, two pounds brown sugar, one-half pound mustard seed, two table-spoons each of cinnamon, cloves, allspice, ginger and ground mustard. Put all together and boil fifteen minutes.

TOMATO CATSUP.
Mrs. W. H. Donovan.

Take one bushel firm, ripe tomatoes; wipe them nicely with a damp cloth, cut out cores and put in a porcelain kettle. Place over fire and pour over them three pints water; throw in two handfuls peach leaves with ten or twelve onions cut fine. Boil until tomatoes are done, which will take about two hours. Strain through a coarse sieve, pour liquid back into kettle, and add one-half gallon good cider vinegar. Have ready two ounces each of ground spice, black pepper and mustard, one ounce ground cloves, two grated nutmegs, two pounds light brown sugar, and one pint salt. Mix these ingredients well before putting into boiler, then boil two hours, stirring continually; add Cayenne pepper if you like. When cool, fill bottles, cork and seal. Keep in cool, dry place.

HIGDEN PICKLES.
Mrs. E. S. Holmes.

One-half bushel green tomatoes chopped fine, one dozen onions, one dozen peppers, sprinkle with one pint salt and let stand over night. In the morning, drain, cover with vinegar and cook slowly one hour; drain again and add two table-spoons each of ground cinnamon and cloves, two pounds sugar, one-half cup mustard. Cover with cold vinegar.

CUCUMBER CATSUP.
Mrs. W. H. Donovan.

Three dozen cucumbers, and eighteen onions peeled and chopped fine; sprinkle over them three-fourths pint salt. Put the whole in a sieve and let drain over night; add one tea-cup mustard seed, one-half tea-cup ground black pepper. Mix well, and cover with good cider vinegar.

PICKLED GREEN TOMATOES AND ONIONS.
Mrs. Paul McCormick.

Chop one peck green tomatoes and one-half peck onions. Let stand two days in layers of salt. Bring to boiling point just enough vinegar to cover. Put in vegetables mixed with one ounce each of cloves and allspice, two ounces white mustard seed, five large red peppers. When well scalded, put in jars.

PICALLILO.
Mrs. L. M. Birely.

Take equal parts tomatoes and cabbage, and chop very fine; white mustard and celery seeds in the proportion of one table-spoon of each to one gallon of vegetables, one table-spoon salt, one-half tea-cup sugar. Cover with vinegar.

CURRANT CATSUP.
Mrs. Philip M. Gallaher.
Five pounds currants, three pounds sugar, one pint vinegar, one table-spoon each of allspice, cinnamon, and cloves, one-half table-spoon each of salt and pepper. Boil two hours over slow fire.

CHOW CHOW.
Mrs. A. J. Wilkinson.
One quart large cucumbers, peeled and cut into strips lengthwise, one quart small cucumbers used as whole pickles, one quart small onions, one quart green tomatoes sliced, one large cauliflower separated into small pieces, six green peppers quartered. Put in a weak brine and let stand twenty-four hours. Scald in the same brine and drain.

Paste—to pour over after scalding: Six table-spoons mustard, one table-spoon tumeric, one and one-half cups sugar, one cup flour, two quarts vinegar. Scald a few minutes, stirring constantly; turn over the pickles and bottle.

SWEET PICKLES.
Mrs. J. F. Sleeper.
Three pounds sugar, one-half pint vinegar, spices to taste. Boil the syrup and pour over seven pounds of fruit.

GRAPE CATSUP.
Mrs. J. A. Johnston, Emporium, Pa.
Five pounds grapes, boil, strain through sieve, and add three pounds sugar, two table-spoons all kinds spice, and two-thirds tea-spoon Cayenne pepper. Boil to the consistency of catsup.

EARLY PICKLE.
Mrs. Rachel Stephenson.
Take small cucumbers off the vine and put in salt water over night. Boil vinegar, sugar and spices, and pour over cucumbers. Put up either air tight or in jars and they will keep green.

WATERMELON PICKLE.
Mrs. L. M. Birely.
Cut rind and red parts off the melon, cut into one or two inch pieces. Take three pints sugar to one gallon melon. Put the melon in vinegar, sugar and spices, and cook to a nice syrup.

CHILLI SAUCE.
Mrs. H. M. Allen.
Twelve large ripe tomatoes, two onions, two red peppers; chop very fine and add one coffee-cup vinegar, two table-spoons sugar, one table-spoon each of salt and ground cinnamon, one tea-spoon cloves. Boil slowly two and one-half hours.

CONFECTIONERY.

CARAMEL FOR COLORING.
Mrs. G. W. Shoemaker.

One cup sugar, one-fourth cup water; let boil until syrup begins to change color, then watch it carefully; tilt saucepan from all sides so it may get equally brown. The moment it is nearly all black, put to it one cup boiling water. Let boil until it is all dissolved like very dark syrup. One tea-spoon of this will make a fine color to gravy, syrup, cake and custard.

CHOCOLATE CANDY.
Mrs. Philip M. Gallaher.

Two large cups brown sugar, one large tea-spoon butter, one-half cup water, one large cup grated chocolate. Pour thin upon buttered plates, and when nearly cold, score into squares.

FRENCH CREAM CANDY.
Mrs. M. J. Crampton.

Break whites of two eggs into bowl and beat slightly; add one-half tumbler cold water, sift and stir in enough confectioner's sugar to make paste stiff enough to mould into shapes with fingers. This is the basis of all cream candy made without boiling.

PEPPERMINT DROPS.
Miss Bertha Crowe.

Two cups sugar, one cup boiling water; boil eight minutes without stirring. When taken from the dish, add eight drops oil of peppermint, then beat with a spoon about five minutes, or until it is white and thick, then drop on buttered papers soon as possible.

ICE-CREAM CANDY.
Mrs. Philip M. Gallaher.

Three cups granulated sugar, one and one-half cups water, one-half cup vinegar. Boil until it hardens in water (not too hard), put in piece of butter size of a walnut, and one tea-spoon vanilla. Pour in buttered plates to cool, then pull until white. Do not stir while cooking.

CHOCOLATE CARAMELS.
Mrs. J. F. Sleeper.

One cup each of chocolate, milk, sugar and molasses, a little butter.

MAPLE CREAMS.
Mrs. J. E. Free.

One cup brown sugar, one cup syrup, one-half cup cream, one table-spoon butter, one tea-spoon vanilla. Boil all together until it begins to harden in cold water; take off the stove and stir until it becomes a waxen substance; then make into balls and put halves of English walnuts on either side. Put on buttered plates to cool.

CHOCOLATE SYRUP.
Maria Parloa.

Into a granite saucepan put one ounce Baker's chocolate, and gradually pour on it one-half pint water, stirring all the time. Place over the fire and stir until the chocolate is dissolved; then add one pint granulated sugar and stir until it begins to boil. Cook for three minutes longer, strain, and when cool, add one table-spoon vanilla. Bottle and keep in cool place.

POP-CORN BALLS.
Miss Hattie Babcock.

Pop as much corn as desired and pick over carefully, taking out all grains burned or not popped. Put on the stove in a pan, about one pint syrup and three large spoons sugar, to a dozen balls, and cook until it becomes a little brittle when put in cold water. Pour syrup over the corn, grease your hands with butter, and immediately make into balls. Use fancy or honey drips for the syrup.

FRENCH CHOCOLATE CREAMS.
Mrs. J. W. Fish.

Two cups granulated sugar, one-half cup milk or water, boil hard five minutes; flavor with vanilla. Stir briskly until it creams sufficient to mould into sizes desired. Dissolve Baker's chocolate over steam, then drop in, one at a time, until covered with chocolate Lay on platter to dry.

MOLASSES CANDY.
Mrs. Love Dill, Brooklyn, N. Y.

One pint molasses, one pint peanuts, lump of butter size of a walnut, one cup sugar (granulated preferred), one tea-spoon soda. Boil molasses until it ropes slightly, then add sugar and butter, cook until done, then add the peanuts and soda; stir quickly and immediately pour upon buttered plates. The peanuts should be cut up or powdered.

MOLASSSES CANDY.
Mrs. J. W. Vaughn.

One quart molasses, one-fourth pound each of butter and brown sugar, two table-spoons lemon extract. Let the molasses boil, put in sugar, when half done, put in the butter and boil one hour. Add the lemon when taken from stove.

WHITE CANDY.
Miss Love Crampton.

One quart granulated sugar, one pint water, two table-spoons vinegar. Boil like molasses candy, but do not stir it. When it becomes brittle in cold water, it is done. Pull same as molasses candy.

FROZEN DESSERTS.

ICE CREAM.
Mrs. J. E. Free.

For a four quart freezer. Three quarts cream, if it is thin; if thick, two quarts cream and one quart milk. Make quite sweet, and any flavor desired. If strawberry flavoring is used, take one quart berries, mash very fine, and sweeten before putting into the freezer. If banana is desired, mash and strain through a cloth.

ICE CREAM WITH GELATINE.
From "Highland Brand Booklet."

One pint Highland Brand evaporated cream, one quart milk, eight eggs, one and one-half cups sugar, one-fourth box gelatine soaked in one-half cup cold milk; heat remainder of milk and cream, beat eggs until creamy, add sugar and beat again, and add the hot cream; then put into a boiler and stir constantly until it thickens; add the soaked gelatine, and more sugar if not sweet enough; strain, and set away to cool. When cold, flavor and freeze.

WATER ICE.
Mrs. J. E. Free.

To one quart strained juice of any fruit, add two quarts water, three pounds sugar, and freeze.

ORANGE ICE.
Mrs. Philip M. Gallaher.

The juice of six oranges and two lemons, mixed with one pint cold water in which has been dissolved one quart sugar; freeze like ice cream.

COMPOTE OF ORANGES.

One dozen oranges, one pound sugar, juice of one-fourth lemon, and one gill water. Boil water and sugar five minutes, skim and add lemon juice. Peel and cut oranges into halves lengthwise; dip a few pieces at a time into the syrup, and lay them on a flat dish (treat all the same), pour syrup over them and set on ice to cool. When ready to serve, place the pudding on a dish, and heap the oranges and syrup on top and around.

GRAPE ICE.
From "The Ladies' Home Journal."

One cup ripe Concord grapes, one pound sugar, one quart water, whites of four eggs. Mash the raw grapes and sugar together, add juice of one lemon; strain into freezer at once.

FROZEN COFFEE CUSTARD.
From "The Delineator."

One-half pound sugar, one-half pint cream, four eggs, one pint milk, one-half pint strong coffee. Set milk upon stove in double boiler to scald. Beat eggs and sugar until very light, and add to the hot milk; cook for an instant, remove from fire, and add cream and coffee. Let the custard cool, then freeze.

NEAPOLITAN ICE-CREAM.
Miss Martha Shoemaker.

One quart milk, one pint cream, yolks of six or eight eggs, one cup sugar, one large table-spoon vanilla. Make a boiled custard of the milk, sugar and yolks of eggs; when cooked, strain, and when cool, add the cream; flavor.

ICED RICE PUDDING WITH COMPOTE OF ORANGES.
From "The Delineator."

To one-half cup rice, allow one pint milk, one quart cream, two cups sugar, yolks of six eggs, one table-spoon vanilla. Cook rice one-half hour in one pint cold water, drain and press through a sieve. Whip the cream, and set in a cold place until wanted. Beat yolks of eggs and sugar until light, and add to the rice. Cook until it thickens, add vanilla, and when cool, freeze. When frozen, add the whipped cream, remove dasher, and let stand in freezer two hours.

STRAWBERRY SHERBET.
Miss Martha Shoemaker.

One quart each of berries, sugar and water, four lemons, one table-spoon gelatine or white of one egg; add the beaten white when partly frozen.

BEVERAGES.

BREAKFAST COCOA.
MARIA PARLOA.

For six cups, use two table-spoons each of powdered cocoa and sugar, one-half pint boiling water, one and one-half pints milk. Put milk on the stove in a double boiler. Put sugar and cocoa in a saucepan, and gradually pour the hot water upon them, stirring all the time. Place saucepan over fire and stir until the contents boil five minutes, then add boiling milk and serve. One gill cream is a great addition to the cocoa.

TEA.
MISS MARTHA SHOEMAKER.

One tea-spoon tea, one cup freshly boiling water. Steam five minutes in an earthen tea-pot. Scald the tea-pot, put in the tea and pour on the boiling water. Cover closely and place where it will keep hot but not boil, for five minutes.

COFFEE.
MRS. RACHEL STEPHENSON.

For six cups, take twelve table-spoons coffee, white of one egg, and boil hard five minutes, then set on back of stove.

A REFRESHING DRINK.
MARIA PARLOA.

Put into a tumbler about two table-spoons broken ice, two table-spoons chocolate syrup, three table-spoons whipped cream, one gill milk, one-half gill soda or Apolinaris water. Stir well before drinking. One table-spoon vanilla ice-cream is an addition. A delicious drink is made by using the syrup, one and one-half gills milk, the ice, and shaking well.

MISCELLANEOUS.

—Kerosene will remove blood stains.

—Egg stains can be removed from silver with damp salt.

—Eggs covered when frying, will cook much more evenly.

—If you heat your knife, you can cut hot bread as smoothly as cold.

—A cup of water set in the oven will keep anything from burning.

—Two apples in a cake box will keep cake fresh a long time. When apples wither, change them.

—To keep glass from breaking when anything hot is poured into it, wrap a damp cloth around it.

—A large slice of potato in the fat while frying doughnuts, will prevent the black specks from appearing on their surface.

—To extract paint from silk or woolen goods, saturate the spots with turpentine and let it remain several hours, then rub between the hands.

—To remove fruit, coffee or tea stains, hold the spot over a pail and pour boiling water from a considerable height through it. Soap sets the stains and should never be allowed to touch them.

—To wash flannels so they will not shrink, wash them in warm, soapy water, but never rub soap on; rinse in warm blue water, and hang in house to dry, never out doors. Have room of same temperature as water in which flannels were washed.

—To change feathers from one bed to another, or from a bed to pillows, open the feather bed as far as the pillow is open, first having pushed the feathers into one corner, away from the opening. Then baste the two open places together, and push the feathers into the pillow. Baste again, then rip first basting, and the work is done with no feathers flying around. This work can be done in the house.

CAMPHOR ICE.

Two ounces each of almond oil and spermaceti, one ounce each of camphor gum and white wax melted together.

HOME-MADE SOAP.

Save grease until you have a five pound pail full, then put over fire to melt, and strain it. At the same time, put one can Babbitt's lye in one quart water and stir until all is dissolved. When cool, pour into the grease slowly, stirring all the time; when this is cool, mark off into cakes. It takes about fifteen minutes to make this soap.

BLACK INK.

Two ounces logwood, one-half ounce each of bi-carbonate potash and copperas, dissolved in one gallon hot water.

LIQUID GLUE.

Dissolve one pound glue in six quarts water, and add two pounds acetic acid.

HOUSEWIFE'S TABLE.

One pound of wheat flour,	One quart.
Indian Meal, one pound two ounces,	One quart.
Butter, when soft, one pound,	One quart.
Ten eggs,	One pound.
Loaf sugar, (broken) one pound,	One quart.
White sugar, one pound one ounce,	One quart.
Brown sugar, one pound two ounces,	One quart.
Sixteen large table-spoons,	One-half pint.
A common sized tumbler,	One-half pint.
One tea-cup holds	One gill.
One large table-spoon equals	One-half ounce.
Forty drops equals	One tea-spoon.
Four tea-spoons equals	One table-spoon.

McIntire Mercantile Co.,
THE CASH TRADERS OF BILLINGS, MONTANA,
Dry Goods, Boots and Shoes, Men's Furnishings!

Bought from first hands for cash, marked at the Lowest Possible Price consistent with business principles, and offered to the people of Yellowstone County for

CASH.

We are Agents for "NEW HOME" and "WHITE" SEWING MACHINES.

CARPETS, RUGS, OIL CLOTHS, MATTINGS, CURTAINS AND UPHOLSTERY GOODS.

Our stock of goods for Men and Women's wear, is always complete for either large or small orders. Try the Cash System and save ten to twenty per cent. on your purchases.

P. S.---Just one request, don't send East for your supplies until you get our prices. Is not this a fair and reasonable request?

McINTIRE MERCANTILE CO., Billings, Mont.

"EASY" TO SWEEP — BEATS A BROOM

Use any of our highest-grade durable sweepers "EASY," "ACME," "IMPERIAL," "SUPREME," "GILT EDGE."

POINTS ON THE "EASY."

Has the celebrated Cam Movement, adjusting the Brush to all grades of carpet by simply raising or lowering the handle while in operation, doing away with the labor of pressing the Sweeper down in order to do good work, making it, as it is named, the Easiest running Sweeper on the market. It has our Common Sense Dumping Device; all you have to do to dump, is press lightly on the lever; no necessity to hold the pans open.

CATALOGUE FREE. If your dealer does not keep the Goshen Sweeper, send us your order and we will have it filled.

GOSHEN SWEEPER CO., Grand Rapids, Mich.

ATWOOD & STEELE'S
DOUBLE
Flavoring Extracts!

VANILLA, LEMON, ETC.

Are the VERY BEST Goods in the Market, and are Unexcelled for Purity and Strength, and Delicacy of Flavor.

FOR SALE BY ALL FIRST-CLASS GROCERS
EVERYWHERE.

FOR THE BEST RESULTS IN YOUR COOKING, INSIST ON USING OUR EXTRACTS.

ATWOOD & STEELE, Chicago.

**COOPER'S
CELEBRATED WAGONS,
BUCKEYE
MOWERS AND BINDERS**

P. YEGEN & CO.,

GROCERIES & PROVISIONS,

Dry Goods and Men's Furnishings,

OATS, BALED HAY AND GRASS SEEDS.

NEW STONE STORE, SOUTH SIDE R. R.,
OPPOSITE PASSENGER DEPOT.

BILLINGS, MONTANA.

SHELF AND HEAVY
HARDWARE.

AGRICULTURAL IMPLEMENTS.

SCHUNEMAN AND EVANS,

SIXTH AND WABASHA STS., ST. PAUL, MINN.

LARGEST RETAIL ESTABLISHMENT
IN THE NORTHWEST.

SIX FLOORS,
   FIVE ACRES OF SELLING SPACE.
   58 DEPARTMENTS.

We sell everything necessary to Clothe Man, Woman and Child from head to foot; to Furnish a Home from Parlor to Kitchen; and many things besides. If you are too far away to come,

SEND FOR OUR LARGE

CATALOGUE,

MAILED FREE TO ANY ADDRESS,
OUTSIDE OF ST. PAUL AND MINNEAPOLIS.

SCHUNEMAN & EVANS,
ST. PAUL, MINN.

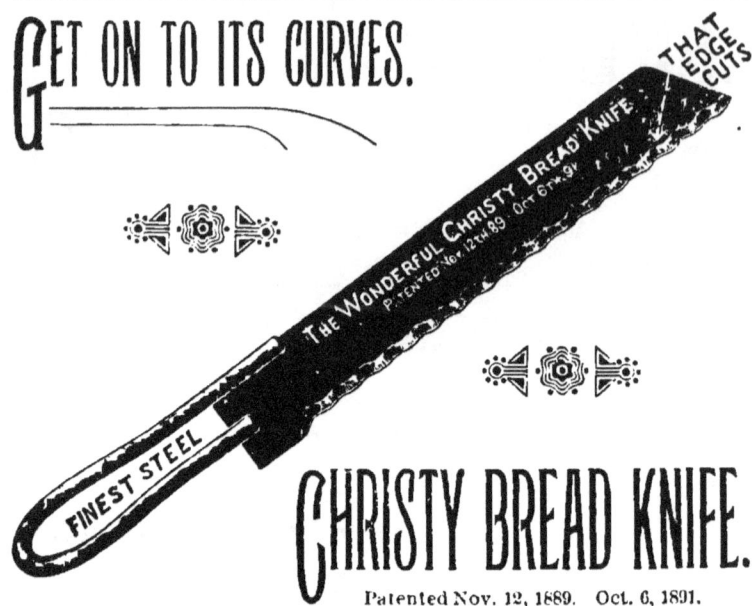

GET ON TO ITS CURVES.

CHRISTY BREAD KNIFE.

Patented Nov. 12, 1889. Oct. 6, 1891.

(SIZE 14¾ INCHES LONG, BY 1½ INCHES WIDE.)

This knife is in a class by itself.
Nothing approaches it in point of
efficacy, durability and simplicity.
It is indispensable
to good housekeeping.
From tip to tip it is solid steel
of finest quality, beautifully finished
and plated.
It is not a machine, but a knife.
Sharpened exactly like any other
knife, on a whetstone or steel.
Cuts thick or thin slices, hot or cold.
No wood or bone connected with this
wonderful knife.
Shall we send you one at our expense
of express or mail, for
seventy-five cents?
You can return it the same way and
get your money if you don't want it.
Agents make fortunes.
Not at stores.
Exclusive territory.
Write us.

CHRISTY KNIFE CO., Fremont, Ohio.

☞ No Chemicals. ☜

W. BAKER & CO.'S

Breakfast Cocoa

Is absolutely pure and it is soluble.

To increase the solubility of the powdered cocoa, various expedients are employed, most of them being based upon the action of some alkali, potash, soda or even ammonia. Cocoa which has been prepared by one of these chemical processes can usually be recognized at once by the distinct alkaline reaction of the infusion in water.

W. Baker & Co.'s Breakfast Cocoa is manufactured from the first stage to the last by perfect mechanical processes, **no chemical being used in its preparation.** By one of the most ingenious of these mechanical processes the greatest degree of fineness is secured without the sacrifice of the attractive and beautiful red color which is characteristic of an absolutely pure and natural cocoa.

W. Baker & Co., Dorchester, Mass.

MANNHEIMER BROS.,
ST. PAUL, MINNESOTA,

Have removed from Third Street to their New Building on the

CORNER OF SIXTH AND ROBERT STREETS.

The stock has been much enlarged, and now exceeds in extent and variety any Dry Goods House in the United States, with the exception of a few of the oldest of the Eastern houses.

We invite special attention to our unparalleled variety of Twilled and Plain

Printed India Silks.

EXTREME NOVELTIES IN FINE WOOL AND SILK MIXED

DRESS FABRICS.

OUR CLOAK DEPARTMENT IS ONE THE LARGEST
in America, and is full of handsome novelties in Coats, Capes, and Costumes for Spring and Summer Wear. Large and Representative Departments for

MILLINERY,
CARPETS,
DRAPERIES,

ART FURNITURE AND UPHOLSTERY,

have been opened, which it is intended shall occupy a leading place in the business of the Northwest.

OUR MAIL ORDER DEPARTMENT

Has been increased in efficiency. Orders are filled with the utmost care and promptness, and invariably at our **Lowest Prices.**

Sixth and Robert Streets, St. Paul, Minnesota.

Important Home-Made Foods
FOR INFANTS AND INVALIDS.

WHEY } *Made with Fairchild's*
JUNKET } *Essence of Pepsine.*

WHEY

Milk freed from its caseine and containing all its other constituents in solution; milk, sugar, fat, soluble albuminoids, mineral salts, etc. Admirable as a temporary food for infants in cases where whole milk is likely to undergo fermentation, owing to disordered condition of the digestive tract.

In these cases, Whey is found to afford adequate nutrition and rest to the digestive functions, and thus presents a most favorable adjunct to medicinal treatment.

JUNKET

A delicious jelly-like curd from milk, acceptable and digestible for patients who are tired of fluid foods, and giving the sense of substance so grateful to convalescents.

Send for *PRACTICAL RECIPES* for making pre-digested foods for the sick, with our especially devised digestive preparations.

FAIRCHILD BROS. & FOSTER,
82 AND 84 FULTON ST.   NEW YORK CITY.

MANNHEIMER BROS.,
ST. PAUL, MINNESOTA,

Have removed from Third Street to their New Building on the

CORNER OF SIXTH AND ROBERT STREETS.

The stock has been much enlarged, and now exceeds in extent and variety any Dry Goods House in the United States, with the exception of a few of the oldest of the Eastern houses.

We invite special attention to our unparalleled variety of Twilled and Plain

Printed India Silks.

EXTREME NOVELTIES IN FINE WOOL AND SILK MIXED

DRESS FABRICS.

OUR CLOAK DEPARTMENT IS ONE THE LARGEST in America, and is full of handsome novelties in Coats, Capes, and Costumes for Spring and Summer Wear. Large and Representative Departments for

MILLINERY,
CARPETS,
DRAPERIES,
ART FURNITURE AND UPHOLSTERY,

have been opened, which it is intended shall occupy a leading place in the business of the Northwest.

OUR MAIL ORDER DEPARTMENT

Has been increased in efficiency. Orders are filled with the utmost care and promptness, and invariably at our Lowest Prices.

Sixth and Robert Streets, St. Paul, Minnesota.

Important Home-Made Foods
FOR INFANTS AND INVALIDS.

WHEY } *Made with Fairchild's*
JUNKET } *Essence of Pepsine.*

WHEY

Milk freed from its caseine and containing all its other constituents in solution; milk, sugar, fat, soluble albuminoids, mineral salts, etc. Admirable as a temporary food for infants in cases where whole milk is likely to undergo fermentation, owing to disordered condition of the digestive tract.

In these cases, Whey is found to afford adequate nutrition and rest to the digestive functions, and thus presents a most favorable adjunct to medicinal treatment.

JUNKET

A delicious jelly-like curd from milk, acceptable and digestible for patients who are tired of fluid foods, and giving the sense of substance so grateful to convalescents.

Send for PRACTICAL RECIPES for making pre-digested foods for the sick, with our especially devised digestive preparations.

FAIRCHILD BROS. & FOSTER,
82 AND 84 FULTON ST.   NEW YORK CITY.

THE Yellowstone Institute!

FOR THE TREATMENT OF

THE { LIQUOR, MORPHINE, TOBACCO } HABIT

THE HIGH ALTITUDE OF BILLINGS, MONTANA, MAKES THIS AN IDEAL LOCATION.

Habitues can have the benefit of the climate, the scenery of the Yellowstone Valley, sound sleep and healthful exercise, in their fight for liberty. For Terms, Etc., Address P. O. Box 403.

www.ingramcontent.com/pod-product-compliance
Lightning Source LLC
Chambersburg PA
CBHW020143170426
43199CB00010B/858